Awards

2012 Eric Hoffer Book Award

2012 First Horizon Award

The Eric Hoffer Award for Books
(http://www.hofferaward.com/)

What Experts Say about *The Chinese Dream*

"In a mere two decades China has developed the world's largest middle class. Helen Wang tells that story – and her own – in this wonderfully informative and readable book."

- Joseph Nye, Distinguished Service Professor, Harvard University, the author of *The Future of Power*

"*The Chinese Dream* offers a fascinating look at one of the most dynamic forces shaping our world today. With an engaging personal perspective, Helen Wang makes sense of the rise of a large Chinese middle class, and of those who have profited from that rise or failed to do so. A truly valuable read for anyone who wants to do business in China."

- Gady Epstein, Beijing Correspondent, *The Economist*

"The growth of China's middle class rivals the growth of China's overall economy as a phenomenon with huge implications for the entire world. Whether China will become a more liberal and democratic society, ... whether it will develop a spiritual power to match its material influence — these and other questions are Helen Wang's topic in this fascinating book. It rings true to what I have seen in China and suggests new possibilities."

- James Fallows, National Correspondent of The Atlantic, the author of *Postcards from Tomorrow Square: Reports from China*

"Helen Wang's conversations, her reflections and stories, bring to life the hopes and concerns of China's emerging middle class. An unusual book, very readable and full of insight."

- John Quelch, Professor at Harvard Business School and former Dean of London Business School

"... the most insightful voice that accurately captures the China of today – its promise and peril – ... have a sense of the country's past, but an equally vibrant vision for its future."

- *Asia Times* Online

"Helen Wang takes us through the world of China's middle class with riveting personal stories, and shows us how this important demographic will alter the global economy in the years ahead. A must-read for businesses that want to tap into this enormous market."

- Shaun Rein, the author of *The End of Cheap China*, Founder and Managing Director of China Market Research Group (CMR)

"*The Chinese Dream* tells one of the most important stories of our time – the rise of the world's largest middle class. Helen Wang enlightens us with the possibility of 'unity in diversity'. A comprehensive, and yet easy to read book about modern China."

- Ken Wilcox, Chief Executive Officer, Silicon Valley Bank

"With a fresh look at the development of the new China, Helen Wang offers an engaging, respectfully researched perspective on the world as one entity as she uncovers the importance of communication, cooperation, and collaboration in her eloquent book, *The Chinese Dream*. A captivating read!"

- Cynthia Brian, New York Times bestselling author, TV/Radio personality/ Founder, Be the Star You Are!®

"The Chinese Dream describes countless possibilities for shared growth, on both national and international levels. For those looking to gain a deeper understanding of modern Chinese society, and those looking to prepare for a new age of globalized collaboration, Helen Wang's *The Chinese Dream* is an exciting and timely resource."

- China Law Blog

"The Chinese Dream ... is the best description in layman's terms of the wildly divergent cultures that must set aside mistrust and misunderstanding in the new one-world global economy."

- The Internet Review of Books

"The Chinese Dream has an obvious resonance with the idea of The Great American Dream."

- China Daily

"The Chinese Dream is enlightening for anyone interested not only in the economic importance of the Chinese middle class today, but also of this group's cultural and political implications for the China of tomorrow."

- Jing Daily

"Helen Wang's book, The Chinese Dream, shows that prosperity and sustainability can go hand in hand. But only if we redefine prosperity for the enormous emerging middle class. Catalyzing this type of sustainable consumerism is what JUCCCE does every day."

- Peggy Liu, Chairperson of JUCCCE,
Time Magazine Hero of the Environment

THE CHINESE DREAM

THE CHINESE DREAM

THE RISE OF THE WORLD'S LARGEST MIDDLE CLASS
AND WHAT IT MEANS TO YOU

HELEN H. WANG

SECOND EDITION

BESTSELLER
BESTSELLER PRESS

BESTSELLER

BESTSELLER PRESS

For information about special discounts for bulk purchases,
please contact info@TheChineseDreamBook.com.

ISBN: 1452898049
ISBN-13: 9781452898049
Library of Congress Control Number: 2010909433

To Paul

For your unconditional love and support

CONTENTS

MAP OF CHINA

FOREWORD

Helen Wang's book represents a powerful contribution to a timely debate about China's role in the world and how changes wrought by her rising middle class will affect us all. In the past the Chinese Dream spoke of centuries of innovation that have given us gunpowder, beautiful ceramics, and gigantic monuments that speak of the Middle Kingdom's civilization, inventiveness and its ability to organize its affairs over a vast land mass and population covering many millions.

The Chinese Dream today as portrayed in Helen's book speaks of a changing China that is discovering consumerism, that is increasingly globalised, and also at a crossroads. Will her path in years to come continue to be one that resembles that of Western countries with all the benefits of further urbanization, wealth, and industrialization, but at the same time challenges in managing scarce resources, population migration, and the social problems that affluence can bring, elsewhere called 'Affluenza'? Or will the Chinese people themselves inside and outside China create a new sustainable Chinese Dream, based on their ancient values of respect for culture, family, and nature, harnessing technology and creativity?

Only time will tell, but Helen's book gives insights into how middle class Chinese consumers are thinking, what they are buying, and the lifestyle pressures they are facing which hints at the possible paths ahead. Over time the symbols of the Chinese Dream will emerge, just as red pillar boxes and the English countryside did for the British Dream in the 19th century and white picket fences and jeans have for the American Dream in the 20th century. The enduring symbols of the Chinese Dream are being invented at this very moment in time.

Above all, and whichever Dream emerges, Helen's book is a reminder of how China's destiny and that of the rest of the world are now inextricably linked, in a Oneness, that can no longer be ignored. To act in ignorance of this interdependence could tear the world apart; embracing it on the other hand may provide a way out of the many challenges we face in the early 21st century. If Chinese and non-Chinese can build on their mutual strengths and come up with innovative solutions that bring together the best of the East and the West then we will all increasingly benefit from the Chinese Dream.

Lord Wei of Shoreditch

PREFACE

In January 1989, I came to the United States to pursue my graduate study. Like thousands of Chinese students, I was coming to America not merely for a chance at academic advancement. It was a way to seek a better future in this "land of opportunity" and "country of freedom." Today, these phrases sound more like clichés. Yet, for those of us who had not known the meanings of words like "opportunity" or "freedom," America was a place for the impossible, a romantic version of what the world was not, and a fantasy land with the glittering skyline of New York City, wild cowboys in California, and humming boatmen on the Mississippi River.

For me, America was a dream coming true.

Shortly after I arrived, I went on a school-organized field trip to Washington, D.C., for a conference. The world was still in the grip of the Cold War. Even to this day, I still cannot fully grasp what it meant for me, who grew up in a country that viewed the United States as an enemy. I visited the White House, national museums, and memorial parks. The chilly winter air could not inhibit my exuberance. As I stood at the Lincoln Memorial and read the Gettysburg Address, the reality that I was *really* in a free country finally hit me. I found myself at a loss for words and overwhelmed by my emotions. I remember the afternoon sunlight casting long shadows in the Lincoln Memorial, flocks of birds flying freely above the Reflecting Pool, and the view of the capital from the top of the Washington Monument.

Later that afternoon, I took a walk on the National Mall. Along the way, I sat on a bench and was about to eat a sandwich I bought from a street vendor. I was thrilled to see birds flying closely around me, as if they were enjoying freedom with me. Some of them landed on the ground, picking up leftover food. Suddenly, a bird dove toward me. Before I realized, it grabbed a big chunk of my sandwich and flew away. I was dumbfounded. "This is indeed a country of freedom," I thought to myself. "Even a bird can pick on me."

In China, this would be impossible. All the birds are afraid of people. They would never dare to be near any person, not to mention trying to rob food from a human's hand. Otherwise, they would likely end up on someone's dinner table. I remember seeing a boy catch a bird in a wicked way and cook it for his meal.

It had happened in winter. Light snow covered the fields outside the compound where we lived. The boy must have been around fifteen at that time, because we teased him for the sparse new hairs on his upper lip. We called him Big Brother, as he was the oldest and acted as a "pack leader" among us. However, in secret, we called him "Little Mustache." I saw Little Mustache wrap the poor bird in chunks of wet mud and choke it to death. Then he threw it onto a hot coal stove and cooked it for his dinner.

We were all nervous and excited, screaming and jumping around as we watched Little Mustache roast the bird. It did not occur to any of us that this was inhumane, cruel, or perhaps a violation of the animal's rights. In a country where food was rationed, some people were starving, and eating meat was a rare treat, the concept of protecting animals, or the environment for that matter, was then nonexistent.

The bird snatching my sandwich was my first taste of freedom in America.

Today, twenty years later, China has changed into a very different country. Each time I have gone back, I have seen amazing changes. Its cities are bigger, and its skylines are more impressive; more things are happening there than in any other part of the world. It struck me that when I left China twenty years ago, there was no Chinese dream. I had to leave my country and come to America in order to pursue my dreams of a better future. But today, many young people in China can start their own businesses and they have a lot more opportunities.

In the meantime, I have found an increasing fear in the West of China's spectacular growth. While some fears might be legitimate, most are unrealistic or due to misunderstanding or mistrust. These fears can be self-fulfilling prophecies and they are a source of global instability. As a Chinese native and an American citizen, I feel compelled to bridge the gap in understanding between China and the West. I believe that the world's stability and prosperity will depend on how well China and the West understand each other, trust each other, and learn from each other.

The main theme of this book, the *oneness of the world*, grows out of my twenty years of experience living at the crossroads of East and West. My experience straddling two cultures allows me to transcend some of my limitations and gain perspective from both worlds. I understand that the *oneness of the world* is not a conventional view readily accepted by Western audiences. However, I invite you to be open to the idea, and walk with me on this journey, which I promise you will find enlightening and rewarding.

My interest in China and its relationship with the West goes back to my graduate work at Stanford University, where the *Stanford Journal of International Affairs* published my paper about China's role in world trade. As a research manager at the prestigious think tank Institute for the Future, I learned invaluable tools and research methodologies that were extremely useful in writing this book. As an entrepreneur in Silicon Valley, I was able to establish an extensive network of contacts, which allows me to access many academic and industrial luminaries.

In writing this book, I interviewed over one hundred people in China and spoke to leading economists and China experts. Because I grew up in China, I have an insider's view of the cultural and social background of current events in China. People in China are more open talking to me than to a foreign journalist. I understand them intrinsically without guesswork. On the other hand, I have lived in the United States for twenty years. I understand the perspectives of American readers and can easily identify some misconceptions people in the West have about China.

Among all the books touching on this subject, the one that most influenced me was Joseph Stiglitz's *Making Globalization Work*. I derived part of my thesis from reading his book. Jonathan Spence's *The Search for Modern China* was an invaluable reference for me on Chinese history. Fareed Zakaria's *The Post-American World* let me see China and its relationship with the West in a larger context. Nick Kristof and Cheryl WuDunn's *China Wakes* deeply impressed me; they effectively presented a complex picture of China by seamlessly integrating stories and arguments. James Fallows's *Postcards from Tomorrow Square* gave me many insights about China. *China: the Balance Sheet,* by the Center for Strategic and International Studies and the Institute for International Economics, was an important resource. Other books that I enjoyed reading include Rob Gifford's *China Road,* James McGregor's *One Billion Customers*, John Pomfret's *Chinese Lessons*, and Zachary Karabell's *Superfusion,* among many others.

Defining the Chinese Middle Class

Defining the Chinese middle class can be confusing, depending on whom you talk to or which numbers you use. The most common definition uses income as a measurement. According to McKinsey Global Institute, the Chinese middle class is those people whose annual incomes, in terms of purchasing power, range from $13,500 to $53,900.[1] The Chinese Academy of Social Sciences (CASS) released a report in 2004 defining the Chinese middle class as families with assets valued from $18,100 to $36,200 (150,000 to 300,000 yuan). The official data from China's National Bureau of Statistics categorize the Chinese middle class as households with an annual income ranging from \$7,250 to \$62,500 (60,000 to 500,000 yuan).

These numbers not only vary, they are also misleading. The cost of living in China is very different from that in the West. For example, a person making \$1,000 a month can have a good standard of living in China, whereas he or she would need some kind of additional assistance in the United States. Even within China, living standards in the major cities, Beijing and Shanghai, are very different from those in smaller inland cities such as Hefei and Kaifeng. A rule of thumb is that middle class people have available one-third of their income for discretionary spending. This group of people has passed the threshold of survival and does not need to worry about the basics such as food and clothing, and has some disposable income to buy discretionary goods and services.

In addition to income measurement, a research team led by Professor Zhou Xiaohong in Nanjing University further defined middle class occupations as professionals in management and technology, entrepreneurs, private business owners, and civil servants (meaning government officials). Unlike in the United States, middle class Chinese are concentrated in large cities. They are also relatively younger than middle class Westerners.

Since "middle class" is a Western concept, to a certain degree, it contains mythical elements for many Chinese. For example, they think middle class Westerners all own homes, drive cars, and travel for vacations. In addition, Chinese believe middle class people should have good manners and a tasteful lifestyle. They do not consider less-skilled professions such as waiting tables as middle class. In China, rural migrants who earn very low salaries mostly fill those jobs.

In *The Chinese Dream*, I use a combination of these definitions: urban professionals and entrepreneurs from all walks of life, who have college degrees and earn an annual income from \$10,000 to \$60,000. Over three hundred million people, or about 25 percent of China's population, met these criteria in 2011.

The Growth of the Chinese Middle Class

Goldman Sachs, the Boston Consulting Group, and McKinsey Global Institute have made predictions for the future growth of the Chinese middle class. The numbers are more or less the same. In this book, I mainly cite predictions from the McKinsey reports "From 'Made in China' to 'Sold in China': The Rise of the Chinese Urban Consumer" and "Meet the 2020 Chinese Consumer."

Based on a proprietary database with data covering the past twenty years, McKinsey uses an econometric forecasting model in combination with interviews in China to predict that the Chinese middle class will reach 612 million by 2025. The key assumption for this prediction is an annual gross domestic product growth rate of 6.5 percent. Even as China's overall economic growth moderates, according to McKinsey, incomes in urban areas will rise faster than GDP because of higher labor productivity and rising education levels.

Some experts believe this prediction is too conservative, and indicate that the Chinese middle class could reach as many as 800 million by 2025.

In addition to economic growth, continuing urbanization will also drive the growth of the Chinese middle class. Another McKinsey report, "Preparing for China's Urban Billion," predicts that China's urban population will expand from 604 million in 2008 to 926 million in 2025, approximately two-thirds of the urban population will be middle class, and the urban economy will generate over 90 percent of China's GDP.

Chapters Preview

The Chinese Dream is organized in two parts. Part One, "The Making of the Middle Class," reviews the dramatic changes over the past fifteen years in China that gave birth to the new breed of Chinese middle class that is still emerging.

The **Introduction** provides an overview of the Chinese middle class and presents the main theme of the book—that the rise of a large Chinese middle class will be a complementary and balancing force in the global community and benefit the world as a whole.

Chapter 1 explores a topic that mystifies many people in the West: how capitalism and communism, two mutually exclusive systems, can exist side by side in China. Through profiles of a state-created bourgeoisie and a communist entrepreneur who wears Playboy shoes and invests in the capitalist stock market, among others, I show how China's not-so-private sector operates. In reflecting on this complexity of Chinese society, I discuss the differences between Eastern and Western ways of thinking and how they, although seemingly contradictory, can be complementary to each other.

Chapter 2 looks at the impact of globalization on the urban Chinese middle class, known as "white collars." Among them are a recruiter who gave up her dream to be a reporter, a gay son of former Red Guards, a blogger who drinks Starbucks coffee and studies American business icons, young entrepreneurs who are becoming increasingly westernized, consuming as fast as the money pours in, and many more. Their stories are a microcosm of modern China, full of the contrast of past and present, the conflict of old and new, and collision of East and West.

Another major factor in the growth of the Chinese middle class is the country's unprecedented urbanization. **Chapter 3** features rural migrants who pulled themselves up out of poverty, examines the reasons for this great migration, and discusses potential obstacles—such as China's rigid household registration and educational systems—to the Chinese middle class's ability to move up. In this chapter, I also debunk the myth of China's manufacturing power and challenge people in the West to see beyond our own immediate interests and view China as an opportunity, rather than a threat.

Part Two, "Complexities and Challenges," discusses the impact of the Chinese middle class on Chinese society, the United States and the rest of the world, how it will change the dynamics of the planet we live in, and why it can lead to a safer and stronger world.

Chapter 4 explores the economic implications of a large Chinese middle class, both for China and for the world. A burgeoning middle class, calculated to reach 600 to 800 million within the next fifteen years, is jumping aboard the consumerism train and riding it for all it's worth—a reality that may provide the answer to America's economic woes. The chapter presents ways Western companies can capitalize on China's enormous consumer market, and argues that the Chinese middle class will be an alternative growth engine for the global economy. As counterpoint to this argument, I deconstruct the myth of China as a superpower.

Although a large Chinese middle class offers significant benefits for the world economy, it will also pose serious challenges to the environment and global warming. **Chapter 5** showcases China's widespread pollution and looks at both the challenges and opportunities presented by this environmental crisis—problems that the West can help solve. The chapter discusses both the bottom-up environmental movement in the West and the top-down governmental approach in China and presents a case for mutual learning and collaboration.

Twenty plus years after Tiananmen Square, will a growing Chinese middle class push for more democracy? In **Chapter 6**, I review China's troubled history of democratic pursuit and interview a former Tiananmen Square demonstrator, an editor for one of China's outspoken magazines, and other intellectuals and entrepreneurs. The chapter discusses the relationship between the Chinese middle class and the government, and explores the possibility of a democratic China.

China is leapfrogging into the information age. **Chapter 7** tells the story of a Chinese Internet entrepreneur who started an e-commerce company that defeated eBay in China. This chapter documents why some companies fail while others thrive in the Chinese market, and illustrates important lessons that multinationals cannot afford to ignore when seeking to do business in China.

China is experiencing a surge in religious beliefs as the country continues to undergo rapid and profound changes. **Chapter 8** recounts stories of people's search for spirituality and their desire to find meaning in life: a jewelry store saleswoman wavering over believing in God, a public relations manager shopping from religion to religion, an entrepreneur who converted to Christianity but is still in doubt, and others. The chapter delves into the government's attitude towards religion and the middle class's quest for balance between material and spiritual enrichment.

The book's **Conclusion** asserts that middle class Chinese and Westerners are connected by a common set of core values and share many of the same aspirations and dreams. By accepting our interdependence and seeking to learn from each other, we will all benefit. The Chinese middle class is an emerging global force that can serve as a catalyst for a more balanced world for all.

Interspersed throughout are my personal stories and life-changing experiences—my childhood in China, my arrival in the United States, and my visits back to China over the years.

Use of Names

The Chinese Dream features many interviews and personal stories. Some of the names are changed to protect individuals' privacy and identities. For personal names, the Chinese convention has the family name first and the given name last, reversing the order in comparison to the Western convention. For example, for *Hu Jintao*, *Hu* is the family name. Most Western media and journalists adopt this convention. When using a Chinese name in an interview or story, I follow the Chinese convention. However, if a Chinese person uses an English name, such as Veronica Chen, I use the Western convention. In addition, the book uses the official pinyin romanization system for well-known places and persons, with a few exceptions for names that are long familiar in the West. Thus, I use the more familiar name of Sun Yet-sen rather than the official version, Sun Yixian.

This book is a nearly three-year labor of love. I hope you find it informative, enjoyable, and enlightening. My wish is that *The Chinese Dream* will help you understand one of the most dynamic forces shaping our world, and prepare you and your children to adapt to a new, competitive landscape of the twenty-first century as it is unfolding.

INTRODUCTION

A Five-Thousand-Year Dream

"When there is harmony in the home, there will be order in the nation.
When there is order in the nation, there will be peace in the world."

– CONFUCIUS

❦

The eighth of August, 2008, was a day that will live in history. It was a day when everything had to go right for the Chinese people. After years of preparation and anticipation, the Twenty-ninth Olympic Games were about to open in Beijing. Everyone in China—grandmas and kindergarteners, housewives and executives, the impoverished and newly rich—took the event as dearly to their hearts as if it were their personal matter. They put on festive clothes, wore beaming smiles, behaved conscientiously, and volunteered for maintaining order and security. "The Olympics is our dream of the century (*Bai Nian Aoyun Meng*)," many said. "Today, it finally comes true."

Hence, people in Beijing willingly gave up driving so that the streets would be less congested. Migrant workers were "asked" to return to their hinterland homes and watch the Games on TVs in their villages. Taxi drivers learned to speak English so they could greet visitors. Factories suspended operations so the air would be cleaner. People refrained from spitting to present a good image of China.

At 8 p.m. local time, billions of people around the world watched in awe the Olympic Opening Ceremony, held in Beijing's new National Stadium, known as the Bird's Nest. As spectacular fireworks in the shape of footprints stepped across Beijing's sky, thousands of performers emerged on stage to create dynamic mosaic movements and sang Confucius's verses "rejoice, friends come from afar." It was a magnificent extravaganza with dramatic choreography and a ravishing presentation. The lucky number eight must have worked magic: the weather was delightful; the wind blew just right; the air smelled of excitement; the lights and colors dazzled eyes; the fireworks were so splendiferous that they looked surreal.

All the spectaculars would not have mattered if it was just a show. It was, rather, a statement from 1.3 billion people who are seeking their place in the world.

The statement started by recapitulating China's five thousand years of history and its ancient civilization. As 2,008 drummers opened the show with a solemn beat, audiences were taken back in time to the height of China's glory. We saw the majesty of the Forbidden City—the colossal red columns, the gleaming yellow roofs, the grand stairways, and the mighty doors all aligned in meticulous geometrical order. A legion of Confucian scholars in striking charcoal-gray and ivory costumes bowed down on their knees to pledge allegiance to one man under heaven—the emperor. A lone dancer, waving a long, emerald-green silk in phantasmagoric form, traversed the Silk Road that first linked China to the West. A group of martial arts performers dressed in white ran around the stadium in a chaotic yet orderly manner, symbolizing the Taoist philosophy that has shaped Chinese thought for ages. Blue-robed oarsmen swayed giant paddles, depicting the seven epic voyages of Zheng He[2] and ancient China's marine prowess. In the background, a grand LED-projected scroll rose wondrously with ink-brushed landscape paintings that were stylized by the dexterous movements of modern dancers.

Until the seventeenth century, China was probably the most advanced civilization in the world. It had established a sophisticated bureaucratic system with an elaborate hierarchy, fortified by Confucian tradition. Its urban and commercial life reached new levels of prosperity. Its arts, culture, and literature were flourishing. Its printing and papermaking technologies were state of the art. Its skills in manufacture of porcelain and silk exceeded anything that could be found in Europe. When Marco Polo traveled to China in the thirteenth century, he saw booming cities, large ships, and holistic herbal medicine. At the time, China's agriculture was more advanced than the West's. Its cities were bigger, people more literate, and ruling classes more meritocratic. It was not surprising that China, meaning "Middle Kingdom" in Chinese, saw itself as the center of the world.

Even today, people in China are still mesmerized by their great past. They speak of their ancient civilization with ardent pride, which may sound pretentious to many foreigners. After all, all the great civilizations on earth are sources of fascination for archaeologists and tourists—mostly because they also had equally great falls.

The fall of China coincided with the rise of the West. By the eighteenth century, China was wrapped up in its hallucination that other nations were peripheral or, using a Chinese word, "barbarian," and too remote from the center of the civilized world to be worthy of attention. While China was asleep, the West underwent the Industrial Revolution and advanced rapidly. In this period, science became a central piece of public discourse in Europe, liberal ideas fermented a notion of democracy that eventually replaced the monarchy, and Adam Smith's economic principles gave birth to modern capitalism.

In the nineteenth century, Western powers expanded their colonies and sought overseas markets for their goods. Lord George McCartney, a British diplomat, led a large delegation to meet Emperor Qianglong,[3] requesting that China open its market for foreign trade. The emperor, however, believed that China had no need for British goods, and spurned them. Thereafter, the British declared war on China to force the self-isolated country to open its ports for their goods.[4] Known as the First Opium War, it was followed by the Second Opium War, and wars with the French and the Portuguese—all ending with humiliating defeats for China.

China had awakened to a much more powerful Western world with modern technology. Disconcerted, the last empire of the Middle Kingdom fell in 1911, ending its five thousand years of glory. However, that did not end China's agony. For nearly one hundred years, one predicament after another paralyzed China: civil wars among warlords, the Japanese invasion in the 1930s, struggles between the communists and nationalists, stagnation during Mao's era after 1949, and the chaos of the Cultural Revolution.[5]

Yet, despite all the suffering and confusion, the dreams of restoring China's greatness never ceased to inspire generations of Chinese thinkers, revolutionaries, and reformers in their quest for a strong China.

Perhaps that is what we saw in the Opening Ceremony of the Olympics: a strong China—a dream dreamed for a century by one billion people that was not meant to die.

As the show continued, we saw a variety of performances of Chinese culture and tradition. While people were impressed with the impeccable presentation, fear also crept into the minds of many Westerners about what a rising China might mean to them. From afar, China's enormous population combined with a fast-growing economy can be intimidating. Its culture and tradition are foreign and enigmatic to many Westerners. For example, people in the West were outraged when they learned that the little girl on stage with a perfect smiling face singing "Ode to the Motherland" was lip-syncing for another girl with a beautiful voice but crooked teeth. Yet, enough Chinese thought it was quite appropriate to sacrifice one's individuality for the "national interest."

In fact, collective interest often overrides individuality in Chinese society. Therefore, with faceless people, a series of gargantuan silver boxes were stacked to build the Great Wall, and then they magically turned into thousands of blooming flowers to symbolize China's opening to the world.

Since 1979, when China embarked on its economic reform, it has dazzled the world with its astonishing growth. In just a quarter of a century, China leaped to become the second largest economy in the world after the United States. For the Chinese people, it was a time of turbulence—a time when things moved so fast that years became days and days became minutes. While hundreds of millions of people arose out of poverty, hundreds of millions more were constantly on the move in search of a better life. It was a time of confusion, too, as China flipped from a self-defeating communist ideology to what seems to be quasi-capitalism, which has problems of its own. Everything turned upside down—what seemed right was wrong and what seemed wrong turned out to be right—and when everything righted itself, still few could fathom the pandemonium.

It has also been a time of great hope and optimism—a time when the most unimaginable things happened. The streets that had been filled with bicycles became jammed with honking Audis and BMWs. New apartment buildings, outfitted with tennis courts and swimming pools, replaced shabby housing blocks. Shopping megamalls vied with one another to rise in metropolitan centers that are far larger than any city in the United States or Europe. Amidst all of this commotion, a new breed of Chinese middle class quietly arrived on the horizon, and will soon change the world as we know it.

That world was epitomized at the climax of the Olympic Opening Ceremony with a giant blue globe rising aloft in the middle of the Bird's Nest stadium. Dancers were circumnavigating between the continents, music was trembling heartstrings, and audiences were electrified with jubilation. We saw the illuminated Olympic rings rising in the arena; we heard the Beijing Games anthem, sung by Sarah Brightman and Chinese pop star Liu Huan at the top of the globe at center stage, with the lyrics: "We are in one world, and we have one dream." Before the Olympic flame was ignited, another round of breathtaking fireworks blazed in the sky above the Bird's Nest. And, somewhere in the background, the Olympic motto, "One World One Dream," seemed to glow, albeit faintly—for now.

"One World One Dream." It seems elusive in today's world, so full of conflict, prejudice, and war. China's rise came at a time when the United States and the other Western countries underwent a series of crises and suffered the biggest recession since the Great Depression. Major events like the Wall Street meltdown, home foreclosures in record numbers, and the bankruptcy of General Motors have taken a serious toll on middle class Westerners. A recent survey by Pew Research Center indicates that majorities in the United States and Europe consider China's growing economy a bad thing for their countries.[6] Apprehensions about China's growing power abound in the West, and they are growing every day.

The Chinese Dream, taking its title from the American Dream and alluding to an easily identifiable concept, shows that many of these fears are misplaced. A portrait of the emerging Chinese middle class, it deconstructs myths about China, and offers an alternative and refreshing view that the rise of the Chinese middle class will be a complementary force in the global community and benefit the world as a whole.

This new middle class, which barely existed a decade ago, will reach the size of more than two Americas in a decade or two. They number in the hundreds of millions, with the same hopes and dreams that you and I have: to have a better life, to give our children an even better life, to have more opportunities, to be close to families and friends, and, hopefully, to share a world that is large enough for all of us. In their stories, we see ourselves—our daily struggles, our passions, and our fears as well as our blessings, and, above all, our spirit that carries us through both good and bad times.

The rising Chinese middle class will play an ever-larger role in China's future growth and change the dynamics of the world we live in. According to studies, by 2020, China will overtake the United States as the largest consumer market in the world.[7] The middle class in China is exclusively urban. In less than two decades, some 300 million people will migrate from rural to urban areas, creating an urban population of approximately one billion, with about two-thirds middle class. China will build an equivalent of ten New York Cities, and over two hundred of China's cities will have more than one million residents.[8]

To understand the immense impact of the Chinese middle class on the global economy, environment, politics, and what it means to all of us, I am going to navigate you through China's fast-changing socioeconomic landscapes—privatization, urbanization, and globalization. In this journey, you will meet many members of the new middle class: home-grown entrepreneurs and executives for foreign-owned firms; connected Communist Party members; rural migrants who lifted themselves up from poverty; an Internet mogul who beat eBay; a gay footwear company manager; a former Tiananmen Square demonstrator; and many more. They share their struggles, hopes, and dreams set against a background of ancient traditions and modern aspirations.

In making sense of these chaotic dynamics, I use a simple metaphor, the *oneness of the world*, to demonstrate why a large Chinese middle class will provide a balancing force for the Western world and become a positive catalyst for greater prosperity and stability in the world. I came to the realization of the *oneness of the world* because of my personal experience. Like many immigrants, when I first came to the United States, I identified with everything American and desired to fit into mainstream American society. I was excited to live my American Dream and went out of my way trying to be a "real American." After years of struggle to reconcile my Chinese roots and Western experience, I realize that "the earth is but one country and mankind its citizens." Whether we are Chinese or Americans, in essence, we are all one human race, like leaves of one tree and waves of one sea.

By "oneness," I mean the interconnectedness, interdependence, and dynamic balance amid diversity that ultimately create a unity. Oneness goes beyond mutual understanding. It requires us to look at not only our own interests, but also the interests of all parties involved. Consider humanity as one human body. We need the different parts of the body—the brain, the heart, the arms and legs—to interact with one another harmoniously to make this "one person" happy and functional. If any of these parts, even as trivial as toes and nails, were hurt, or undeveloped, or malfunctioning, the "one human body" would not be able to enjoy its fullness and wholesomeness. This metaphor and argument are further deepened by my understanding of the paradoxical concept of yin and yang. The cornerstone of Chinese philosophy, these two primal forces, seemingly contradictory to each other, in reality balance and complete each other.

As we journey deep into Chinese society, we will see that the *oneness of the world* is a fitting framework for understanding the rise of the Chinese middle class. In today's global economy, *Oneness in Economy* (chapter 4) is evident as we see that a stimulus package in Beijing could affect jobs in Detroit; the stock market in New York could make or break an entire manufacturing industry in Shenzhen. As the middle class in China grows, its domestic consumption will increase. The Chinese middle class has become and will continue to be a powerful alternative growth engine for Western companies as well as the world economy. It will not only help the Chinese economy to rebalance from its current excessive-saving syndrome, but it will also create opportunities for the American economy to alleviate the pain of overconsumption. When the two major economies with opposite strengths and weaknesses can rectify and fortify each other, the world will be able to thrive on the virtuous cycle of globalization without being vulnerable to an American recession.

While this benefit of the Chinese middle class is promising, the challenge that comes with it is equally daunting. If hundreds of millions of middle class Chinese can afford to drive cars and own homes with modern appliances, it will cause calamitous damage to the environment. In fact, China has already surpassed the United States to become the world's largest energy user and polluter. As globalization has forced the United States and China into an alliance that geopolitics could not have envisioned, global warming may force the United States and China into a partnership despite the distrust between the two countries. In the West, green initiatives are a bottom-up movement as ordinary citizens take the matter into their own hands. In China, it is a top-down approach as the central government responds to the urgency of the problems. Both approaches are needed, and one without the other is inadequate. *Oneness in Environment* (chapter 5) is inevitable as the environmental challenges transcend national boundaries; no country alone can win the battle against global warming.

China's six hundred million to eight hundred million emerging consumers create irresistible opportunities for businesses around the world that want to tap into this enormous market. Multinationals, ranging from retailers to automakers, from online marketplaces to banking and financial services, have already marched into China. In the meantime, competition from local companies is also on the rise. As presented in the eBay-Alibaba case, the mighty global giant made fatal mistakes by neglecting the differences between the U. S. and Chinese markets and lost its battle to a Chinese guerrilla company. *Oneness in Competition* (chapter 7) challenges us to "look at the world upside down" because "if you know both sides, you know the best way."

One of the biggest differences between the East and West is in paradigms of thought. Westerners are inclined to think linearly, which is based on logic. Chinese are more accustomed to reason in a nonlinear fashion, which is derived from intuition. As we will see in the stories of China's privatization, middle class Chinese tend to see events in the world as an evolving process, where changes are inevitable and there is no absolute certainty. Ambiguity is part of who they are. Their thoughts, language, social interactions, and even business structures appear opaque and enigmatic to Westerners. While these differences have the potential to cause misunderstandings, they can also be a source for revelation when we recognize the strengths in both approaches. The difference parallels the complementary functions of the right and left brains, and we really need both. *Oneness in Thought* (chapter 1) urges us to see things from different perspectives and expand our horizons.

Even the cultural differences between the East and West can be complementary rather than conflicting. While Western culture is characterized by individualism, Chinese culture emphasizes collectiveness. Many middle class Chinese are under high peer pressure in career choices, marriage, and consumption preferences. Unlike middle class Westerners, they tend to value national unity more than individual freedom. While younger Chinese are becoming more individualistic, Westerners can also benefit from a greater sense of community and belonging. When either is practiced to an extreme, the result can be malignant; therefore, *Oneness in Culture* (chapter 2) calls for moderation and a balance of the two.

Once we recognize the inevitability of the oneness of the world and embrace its benefits, we will find ourselves in a world that is a lot safer and stronger than we ever imagined. *The Chinese Dream* provides ample evidence that a strong China with a large middle class can give rise to greater stability and prosperity in the world. There will be disruptions as the dynamics of global politics, culture and the environment will be altered. However, if we embrace the principle of unity in diversity as demonstrated throughout this book, we will realize that China's rise does not have to be at the expense of the West. Rather, it reinforces and balances the West—just as a strong Western world reinforces and balances China. If China and the West can learn from each other, trust each other, and cooperate with each other on important international issues, the world will be a much better place for all.

PART I

THE MAKING OF THE MIDDLE CLASS

CHAPTER 1

A Peculiar Private Sector

*"The inherent vice of capitalism is the unequal sharing of blessings;
the inherent virtue of socialism is the equal sharing of miseries."*

– WINSTON CHURCHILL

❧

On one of my many flights from San Francisco to Shanghai, an article in *Fortune* magazine, "China's Mobile Maestro," caught my attention. It described the seemingly impossible task of China Mobile Chief Executive Officer Wang Jianzhou to reconcile the divergent interests of the thousands of shareholders and hundreds of millions of subscribers while pleasing the one Communist Party. Wang, as described in the *Fortune* magazine article, didn't think that dealing with divergent interests was any more confounding than running a regular business. He said, "I don't think it's so difficult to find the balance. As head of a state-owned enterprise, my duty is to maximize the value of state assets. As CEO of a listed company, my job is to enhance value for our shareholders." [9]

China Mobile is the largest state-owned mobile phone company in China, but it is also listed on the New York Stock Exchange. Beginning in the early 1990s, China went through a sweeping privatization of its state-owned enterprises (SOEs), which had been the backbone of the country's economy before the reform.[10] Many large state-owned enterprises were restructured; countless small- and medium-sized state-owned firms were shut down, sold off, or taken over by the managers. While millions lost jobs, millions of others inherited state assets and instantly became financially well-off.

In this transition, a new middle class was being created by the state. In the meantime, privately owned enterprises, which were illegal and mostly nonexistent before the economic reform (1979), grew robustly in every corner of the country and became a significant force behind China's miraculous growth.

I can understand that many people in the West are mystified by the fact that capitalism and communism, two mutually exclusive systems, can coexist in China. I had exactly the same question when I started to write this book. How could China's bureaucratic state enterprises be transformed into bottom-line-driven commercial companies? What happened to make all these seemingly conflicting interests work out well? As a native Chinese, I worked at a state-owned company before I came to the United States for graduate study and, subsequently, had an eventful career in Silicon Valley. It's sufficient to say that I have one foot in each country. I decided to find out on my own.

My Hometown, Hangzhou

My journey naturally started in my hometown, Hangzhou, about 180 miles southwest of Shanghai. Hangzhou is the capital city of Zhejiang province with about six million inhabitants. It is known for a beautiful lake, named West Lake. The lake covers almost three square miles and is surrounded on three sides by wavy, lush hills. It has an exquisite landscape, ornamented by traditional-style pavilions, pagodas, and causeways with arching bridges. Along the lake are plum and willow trees, quivering and whispering in gentle breezes. In the spring, the pink and white blossoms entwine with the green willows, and West Lake looks like a tender bride ready to wed.

Legend has it that over two thousand years ago, West Lake was part of the Qiantang River[11] that flowed into the East China Sea. Due to the sediment of earth, the surrounding mountains gradually stretched to shape a shoal. Eventually, a sandbank between mountains on the north and south sides was built up and a lagoon on the west came into shape, which became West Lake as we know it. China's first emperor, Qin Shi Huang (259 BCE–210 BCE), is said to have sailed down from the East China Sea before the lake was formed and anchored his ship to a giant stone, which can still be seen on the north side of the lake. Throughout history, many poets, philosophers, and statesmen have written mesmerizing poems about West Lake.

I grew up hearing people praise Hangzhou as a "paradise on earth." However, I was oblivious to its charms. The stillness of the lake seemed lifeless to me, and I was desperate to leave the country. Like everyone else, I was brought up to believe that communism was the highest ideal—it was a world without inequality, since all assets and property were collectively owned by all people. We were told that we were lucky to live in a "socialist new China" because we were the masters of the country. According to Karl Marx, socialism is a transitional stage between capitalism and communism. After socialism, society would advance to the next stage, communism, via class struggle. We were also told that people in capitalist countries such as the United States were miserable—they were very poor and exploited by a few rich people. I remembered seeing cartoons of a big-nosed Uncle Sam with captions such as "Down with Capitalism" or "Down with Imperialism."

My memory of the Cultural Revolution was chaotic. My father, an official in the Science and Technology Bureau of Zhejiang province, was quarantined and interrogated for his "conduct" at some point in history. Some of my cousins were sent to the remote countryside for "reeducation." By the end of the Cultural Revolution, most people figured out that something was terribly wrong. A teenager then, I buried myself in a world of books, poetry, and art. Most of the books available in those days were Chinese classics, such as *Dream of the Red Chamber* and ancient poems from the Tang and Song dynasties (618-1279 AD). Western books were banned, but people who were thirsty for knowledge could still find a way to access the hidden treasure of world classics. Among them were Leo Tolstoy's *Anna Karenina* and Charlotte Bronte's *Jane Eyre*. I would spend hours daydreaming in a world that existed only in books. My mother, a nurse with a traditional Chinese mindset, used to shake her head and say, "A girl should be learning to cook and sew, not to read."

By the time I went to college in the 1980s, China was gradually opening up. We still had very little information about the outside world. I majored in English. The course material from England was mostly outdated, with little real-world information. I learned some Shakespearean sonnets, and vocabulary such as "where is the water closet?" (The professor would give a hand signal that indicated "WC.") However, I found some Xerox-copied supplemental class reading materials from the United States fascinating. Among them were Abraham Lincoln's Gettysburg Address and Martin Luther King's "I Have a Dream" speech. It was an epiphany for me. I may not have fully understood the significance of these speeches, but something in them touched me profoundly. I found myself choked up by their power and inspiration. I was never interested in politics and couldn't care less about capitalism or communism. All I knew was that I wanted to go to that great country—"a new nation, conceived in Liberty, and dedicated to the proposition that all men are created equal.... that this nation, under God, shall have a new birth of freedom—and that government of the people, by the people, for the people, shall not perish from the earth."[12]

When I landed a job at a state-owned import and export company, everyone congratulated me. It was the best possible job one could get—prestigious and glamorous, with lifetime job security and good benefits. But my heart and mind were fixated on going to America. I spent weekends in libraries researching universities and graduate schools in the United States, and stayed up late at night preparing for the TOEFL (Test of English as a Foreign Language) and GRE (Graduate Record Examination) exams required to apply to U.S. universities. In the 1980s, only a very few privileged Chinese were able study overseas. Most of them were sent by government-sponsored programs. My chances to be admitted to an American university with a scholarship were next to zero. At the time, it seemed an impossible dream.

A colleague of mine, Xu Xin, was genuinely concerned as he saw my single-minded focus on something I knew very little about while throwing away a life that many envied. With the best intentions, he lectured me on life's greatest wisdom. "You need to be pragmatic," he said. "Life is about *chai-mi-you-yan* (chops, rice, oil, and salt, or the nitty-gritty of everyday life), not about romantic ideas in your head. Have your feet on the ground. Be content with what you have."

That day, I rode my bicycle home in an icy wind that cut into my skin like a knife. The first winter snow began to fall and melted upon touching the ground. The road became slippery as the snow-rain mixed with dirt and animal waste from livestock carts that peasants brought in for sale. I got off the bicycle and began to walk along the side of the road crowded with bicycles and pedestrians. I looked down at my mud-tainted rain boots that were almost worn out. I knew as plain as I could see: my feet *were* on the ground. Had I not read "I Have a Dream," I might have settled for the nitty-gritty of everyday life and been content with my not-so-bad fortune. But "I've been to the mountaintop" and "I've seen the Promised Land," and there was no turning back for me. As I gazed at the sky, dark with heavy clouds ahead of me, I was more determined than ever.

In January 1989, I boarded a plane to San Francisco and began a remarkable new journey in America.

Twenty years passed in a blink of an eye. Today, Hangzhou has changed beyond my recognition. Small alleys have become wide boulevards. The city has almost quadrupled in size, expanding to include the surrounding towns and villages. Even West Lake has been renovated—many historical sites have been developed and new scenic spots added.

Hangzhou would have been a perfect resort town. But in today's bustling China, it has become a hub for private business and entrepreneurship. Its old state-owned enterprises were typically medium and small sized. Most of them were restructured, sold off, or shut down during the privatization process. Unlike the northern part of China, where large state-owned enterprises dominated, Hangzhou's private enterprises had been traditionally active since the early days of the reforms. As a result, these private enterprises were able to act quickly to capitalize on opportunities, absorbing laid-off workers and emerging stronger after the shocks of privatization. Hangzhou has several of the most successful homegrown companies—the country's largest auto parts maker, Wan-Xiang; soft drinks group Wahaha; and e-commerce company Alibaba, which had a phenomenal initial public offering (IPO) of stock in November 2007 that rivaled Google's.

A Sales Manager Becomes an Owner

While in Hangzhou, I met with an old colleague, Chen Ling (not her real name), with whom I shared an office in a state-owned import-export company before I left for the United States. One of the nice things about China is that you can always call someone—no matter how much time has passed since you last saw them—and you'll find yourself among a gathering of old friends, drinking tea in a boutique tea house or having dinner in a three-story restaurant. The Chinese are very gregarious people (they had better be—there are 1.3 billion of them!). So, I called Chen Ling up and invited her over for tea.

It was a typical summer day for Hangzhou—hot and damp with scattered rain. After brief showers, the sun came out expectantly from behind the clouds while straggling rain drops were still falling. The green mountains outside my hotel window were covered with a mysterious haze. The scene reminded me of a Chinese poem: "The sun appears in the east while the rain falls in the west; can you tell me whether it is clear or overcast?" Since the word "clear" can also mean "feeling" in Chinese, and "overcast" "no feeling," the poem is often used to refer to the ambiguity of a situation. To me, the poem says something that is inherently true about China: nothing is ever clearly black and white. Everything in China is obscured.

Chen Ling and I met in my hotel lobby. After almost twenty years, she looked just as I remembered: slender, simple outfit, and no makeup. In her forties, Chen Ling had a classic demeanor known for women in this part of the country, soft and sweet. Her neatly cut hair was much shorter than I remembered. As we sat down for tea, I noticed her half-transparent nylon socks inside her open-toed, high-heeled shoes. Even on such a hot summer day, Chinese women of my generation seldom did pedicures to show off their toes.

While sipping persimmon tea, we chatted to catch up with each other's lives. Chen Ling is one of those people who are always so nice that you know there is much more underneath the niceness. She was sort of coy, observant, and soft-spoken in a disguised, self-deprecating manner that Chinese women often adopt. Her business card said she was "sales director" of Guangda Xindi Co. Ltd., a company that exports frozen food products (the company name is changed to protect its privacy). In reality, she owned 35 percent of the company, which had an impressive sales record.

The History of Privatization

China's privatization can be traced back to 1991, when two stock exchanges, one in Shanghai and another in Shenzhen, were established to "experiment" with market forces. In the early years, selected state-owned enterprises were listed on the stock market to sell a limited quantity of shares to the public. Although the stock market was bound by many restrictions, it soon raised hundreds of billions of equity capital to fund ailing state-owned enterprises.[13] In 1997, the government decided to make greater use of the stock market. As a result, nearly all the restrictions were relaxed step by step. By 2005, more than 1,300 state-owned companies were listed on the stock market, and a total of $270 billion worth of state assets were free to trade.[14] The two exchanges, equipped with computerized trading systems and a nationwide satellite network, became fully functional financial systems. By 2007, the Shanghai and Shenzhen markets were valued at $1.4 trillion, compared to $20 trillion on the New York Stock Exchange.

In the meantime, China's urban state enterprises started ownership restructuring programs. Small- and medium-sized state firms were privatized fully or partially, while large firms operating in key sectors, such as banking, telecom, energy, and media, retained state ownership. The ownership restructuring program is a critical part of privatization and has transformed many state enterprises into shareholding companies. The program offers the managers at state-owned enterprises the opportunity to purchase shares of the companies. It involves estimating the present value of the company's future profit stream. But often, a simple pricing method is applied: the book value of the firm's total assets minus its depreciation and total debts outstanding.[15] Between 2001 and 2006, the number of state-owned enterprises was reduced from 370,000 to 120,000. An estimated five thousand state-owned enterprises are privatized each year.[16] In the process, enormously valuable state assets were transferred legally to individual hands.

The New State-Created Bourgeoisie

In 2000, the company Chen Ling worked for—Guangda International—started the restructuring process. It had seventeen divisions organized along product lines ranging from textiles and apparel to frozen vegetables, and was mostly engaged in the import and export business. The company also had a sideline business in real estate, which is not unusual for a state company in China, especially when it has a strong government connection.

During that time, many people from state-owned companies "jumped into the sea" (gave up their bureaucratic positions) to catch their share of the gold rush. Chen Ling, however, enjoyed working at the state company and valued the stability and prestige it entailed. With her agreeable demeanor, she soon won her boss's favor and was promoted to sales manager for the frozen vegetables division. To be sure, Chen Ling was a diligent and devoted worker. During her tenure, she successfully increased the division's sales more than tenfold within five years.

When the ownership restructuring started, Chen Ling was a natural candidate to take over the division. The plan was that all the managers would be given 30 percent shares of their divisions, which they could pay back with future profits. In return, they would be legally responsible for the profit and loss of the business. This was an incredibly good deal: the division was valued at only $625,000 while it already had sales revenue of $30 million. Chen Ling brought in a partner, who turned out to be a friend of her husband's, to take charge of the production side of the business. The frozen vegetables division changed its name to Guangda Xindi Co. Ltd., with Chen Ling serving as its chairwoman and juridical officer (the person who is held accountable legally for the business).[17]

Similarly, other divisions within Guangda International were also taken over by their managers. By 2001, Guangda International, a state-owned company, became a conglomerate with seventeen subsidiary companies, all of which were partially privately owned by the managers. Over time, more shares were released to the managers and their executive teams, with the state's share shrinking to 30 percent. By 2007, Guangda International was primarily a privately owned company. Its managers owned the majority of its share and the state the minority, with some shares trading on the stock market.

There was no open bidding, no auction, and no initial capital requirement. The process transferred wealth from the state to individuals. Some of them were connected and capable, others were simply in the right place at the right time. The government withdrew from almost all the small- and medium-sized state enterprises. But the government didn't disappear. It only became less visible.

Victims of the Old Socialist System

For every Chen Ling, there were many like Lian Su, who was a laid-off worker. During the privatization process, some managers and corrupt officials simply divided state assets and closed down the companies, leaving thousands of laid-off workers in dismay.

Lian Su was born in 1952 as the first of three children to a family of teachers. Her father named her "Su" after the first Chinese character of "Soviet" (Su Wei Ai). With that name, the father instilled in her infant soul a utopian dream that they would live in an ideal world where there would be no miserable poor people who are being abused, nor evil rich people who exploit the poor. Indeed, that was the dream that sustained millions of people in the 1950s and '60s. Many people devoted their lives to it, and plenty were willing to die for it. However, it didn't take too long for that dream to turn into a nightmare.

Lian Su was fourteen years old when the Cultural Revolution started. Like most youth in those days, she lost her teens when she should have studied in school. At eighteen, she was sent to the countryside of Yunan province in southwest China and spent her twenties growing water rice in a remote village. When the craziness of the Cultural Revolution was finally over, Lian Su married a fellow classmate, returned to the city, and managed to find a stable job in Hangzhou Chemical Factory. Lian Su no longer thought about that utopian dream. In fact, she had forgotten about it, but she did hope to work in the same factory for the rest of her life.

However, that hope did not last long. On a hot summer day, Lian Su showed up at her workplace and found herself being laid off from the factory where she had worked for fifteen years. The manager told her that she was lucky to have a severance pay that was worth about $3,000 because she was a technician. "Others didn't even get this much," he said. Lian Su felt it was like a death penalty. Being laid off in her forties was the worst thing that could happen to her—too early to retire, but too late to start all over again. Could she live on her limited pension? What if she became ill and could not afford mounting medical bills?[18]

Lian Su was among thirty million people who were being laid off. In the West, layoffs are a by-product of economic cycles. In China, however, layoffs were simply not a function of the society. The "socialist iron bowl" system guaranteed everyone a job for lifetime. When the system suddenly disappeared, people were completely disoriented. Most of them were sent home for good with $30 to $80 monthly pay. Many lost their health insurance and pensions. More than anything else, they felt betrayed and abandoned. They felt they had lost and were deprived of something to which they were supposedly entitled—a piece of the country that they once owned.

In any other economy, this level of layoffs and job losses would cause chaos and plunge the country into depression. In China, the economy kept growing by double digits. One of the strong characteristics about China's growing economy is entrepreneurship.

Huang Yong was laid off from an electronic parts factory where he had worked for almost twenty years. Feeling desperate,

Huang went out to the streets, ready to jump into anything that could bring him a few yuan. Within a couple of years, he had sold electric fans and had become a truck driver. He got a job in a private company in charge of a 23,000-square-foot warehouse. However, the company went out of business and he went back to the streets. He grabbed whatever he could get so he wouldn't fall into the abyss of poverty.

Fortunately, opportunities were also abundant. In 2006, Huang learned that a household security company was looking for distributors for its new alarm systems for apartments. Huang borrowed 20,000 yuan ($2,941) from several friends as an initial investment to become a distributor. In the following years, Huang worked seven days a week and did door-to-door sales in countless residential communities. As more and more new apartments were built in the area, Huang's business grew quickly because of increased demand. He hired some people to help him, many of whom were laid-off workers like himself. "Although a small business," he said, "the income is ten times what I earned in a state company."[19]

Many, however, have not been so fortunate. The old socialist safety net has been broken. Laid-off workers often cannot afford to pay for health insurance, whose cost has increased more than tenfold. They also have to tuck away a big chunk of income for retirement, not to mention saving for their children's education. Life has become a constant struggle for them.

Thriving Private Enterprises

When millions of people were laid off from state companies, many of them went into private businesses. In China, private enterprises were not fully legalized until 1997, although the first law permitting private enterprises was passed in 1993. Nevertheless, private enterprises were thriving long before that. Many private businesses "rented" the shell of state-owned companies, but operated completely outside of the government's umbrella. People called this "wearing a red hat." By 2007, private enterprises employed more than two hundred million people and generated two-thirds of China's industrial output.[20]

In this chaotic transition, the people who benefited most were the younger generation born after the Cultural Revolution (1966-1976). Wu Haitao, a young entrepreneur in Hangzhou, is one of them. Wu was engaged in a telecommunications business. Through an introduction from a friend of mine, I met him for lunch.

Wu graciously picked me up in his charcoal-colored Buick Regal. We headed toward Meijia Wu Tea Culture Village, the newly developed area on the west side of West Lake. In the old days, the village was known for its "ten miles of tea terraces." It has since been turned into a maze of teahouses, restaurants, and parks. The peasants who used to grow tea now run big tea businesses. Only a half hour from downtown Hangzhou, the village is a popular place for people to take a midday break.

As we sat down for lunch, Wu lit up a cigarette, not bothering to ask for a lady's permission. He had a slightly heavy build and wore a plaid polo shirt. His black leather shoes had a logo of a bunny wearing a tuxedo bow tie. I knew that Playboy was a U.S. media company that publishes semi-porn magazines mainly for male readers. I did not know that it had product lines such as shoes, belts, and suitcases. It turned out that Playboy's little bunny was as popular as Ralph Lauren's polo rider in China. In the U.S., a *Playboy* magazine is not something people would display in their family rooms, and they would definitely hide it from their children. In China, Playboy shoes and suitcases are something to show off in public.

I remembered that back in Silicon Valley at a conference, a delegate from Hangzhou municipal government proudly presented Hangzhou as a "paradise of Silicon Valley." People in the audience chuckled and shrugged. Not understanding why

Westerners were not impressed, the presenter went on at length to explain why Hangzhou really was a "paradise of Silicon Valley." For readers who are not familiar with Chinese propaganda, the term was used by the officials to brag about their city. The subtext is this: "look, Hangzhou is not only naturally beautiful like a paradise, but also has a lot of technologies like Silicon Valley." The Chinese delegate could not see anything improper in her statement because such oddities have become commonplace in China. I have met people who worked in totally unrelated fields: a university professor running an advertising company, a magazine editor with a venture capital business on the side, and an acclaimed artist holding a high position in government.

A teacher turned entrepreneur, Wu Haitao had experienced the best time in China's recent history. His story sounded like a whirlwind of good fortune. Only ten years before, he earned $50 a month as a lecturer at Hangzhou Metrology College and lived with his parents and grandparents in a 200-square-foot room that they used both as a bedroom and dining room. Opportunities seemed to fall upon him. He soon left his teaching job and joined several partners to form a company. They took on whatever projects that could make money. Now the company has become a multimillion-dollar business with a mixed portfolio, including telecommunications services, education, and entertainment such as automobile racing.

Wu's experience is not unusual for many people in coastal cities. At thirty-three, he already owned two condominiums and was contemplating buying a third. As people accumulated wealth quickly, they poured their cash into real estate because there were no sophisticated financial products for people to invest in. Married and with a young child, Wu Haitao couldn't be more satisfied with his life.

"I think the Communist Party is great," he said.

"Are you a party member?" I asked, a little surprised.

"Yes, I joined the party when I was a senior in college," he said.

"Were you required to study *zibenlun* (*Das Kapital*) when you joined the party?" I asked. *Das Kapital*, by Karl Marx, defines communist theory.

"No," he said. "But only the best students in my class were allowed to join the party."

According to China's state media, Xinhua, more Chinese college students have joined the Communist Party in recent years.[21] At Wu's age, he had never experienced hard times and knew nothing but prosperity. For him and some young people in China, joining the party was a badge of honor. It had little to do with ideology, but a lot to do with status and practical benefits, such as career advancement and good connections in the government. Many new members of the new middle class approve what the government has done. They are business oriented and have a stake in the economy and, therefore, support pro-growth policies.

When I asked Wu about his future plans, he answered like a typical entrepreneur: "I hope to take the company to IPO on the domestic stock market in three years."

"Are there a lot of government restrictions on a private company having an initial public offering on the stock market?" I asked.

"Not as many as people think." He blew smoke rings and grinned, showing his smoke-stained teeth. "The Shanghai and Shenzhen stock exchanges will have an IPO board for privately owned companies next year, and many people want to list their companies on the domestic market."

I was quite amused, wondering how I could possibly explain to my American friends that a Chinese communist entrepreneur who wears a pair of Playboy shoes fancies the capitalist stock market.

On our way back, Wu Haitao appeared more relaxed and started to talk like "words flowing as a river" (speak eloquently).

This chain-smoking, Playboy-shoe-wearing, communist-connected, and capitalist-practicing young man was also a philosopher. "I think Eastern culture is very different from Western culture," he said. "In our Eastern wisdom, there are no absolute right answers for things. It all depends on your own understanding and how enlightened you are. In the West, they use scientific methods, black and white, cause and effect…it's all about logical thinking. But I don't think everything can be understood by logic. In the East, we emphasize balance and harmony."[22]

What Wu said about the differences between the East and West made perfect sense to me. But for the moment, I was enraptured by the winding road lined with willow and firmiana simplex trees. Along the road are many scenic spots and resort areas that I had never seen before, named Home in the Mountain, Bamboo Path at the Cloudy Hills, and Nine Creeks in the Misty Forest. As is characteristic of Hangzhou, all the names chosen for places, old or new, are hopelessly poetic and romantic. I started to recite silently an ancient poem from the famous poet You Lu (1125–1210 BC):

> The hills are stacking and water winding,
> Just as I thought the road is ending,
> Behind the shadowed willows and luminous blooms,
> Yet there is another village hiding.[23]

Sitting in the car, I thought about the unsightly Highway 101 that runs through Silicon Valley, and wondered why on earth anyone in the world would want a "paradise on earth" to be a "paradise of Silicon Valley."

State Capitalism

In today's China, the Communist Party has nothing to do with communist ideology. In fact, the Communist Party of China has become the biggest capitalist. Bill Li, a consultant in Beijing, joked that the Chinese government wears a Polo shirt and Nike shoes, but still has a communist hat. "Someday," he said, "if the government has the courage to throw away that hat, everything will be all right."

Academics coined the term "state capitalism" for China's system. According to Ian Bremmer, author of *The End of the Free Market: Who Wins the War between States and Corporations?*, state capitalism is a system where some major corporations are backed by the state, although they act like private companies. In this system, the state is the leading actor in the economy. The state sets the rules and drives strategic investments in key sectors. This is exactly what is going on in China.

Since the Communist Party is the biggest capitalist, many private businesses consider it a competitive advantage to have a strong government connection in order to leverage huge government resources, such as the funding and branding that they desperately need. Zhu Min, an entrepreneur who started WebEx, an Internet company that provides Web conference services, and returned to China as a venture capitalist, told me that the best business in China is not B-to-B (business to business) or B-to-C (business to consumer), but B-to-G—business to government. The line between public and private cannot be more blurred.

Chery Automobile, a private enterprise invested in by the local government, is a perfect example of the significance of having strong government support in business.

In 1997, a few young men in the small town of Wuhu in Anhui province in central China made an automobile engine, only to find out later that nobody wanted it. With the local government's support, they decided to manufacture a car for the engine, only to discover later that the company didn't have a license to sell cars. After overcoming much red tape, they finally obtained the license and started to sell passenger cars in China. But no one took them seriously because the auto industry was dominated by big-name joint ventures such as Volkswagen and Shanghai Automotive Industry Corporation. Ten years later, however, against all odds,

Chery Automobile grew into one of the major players in the auto industry and ranked fourth among the "Big Five" automakers in China. It also became the top Chinese automobile exporter, with its Tiggo, Easter, and A5 models running on the streets of nearly seventy countries.[24] Chery's success is a combination of luck, perseverance, and, most importantly, government support. It also illustrates China's private sector, which is really neither private nor public.

Since China evolved from a state-controlled socialist system to a semi-market economy with capitalist attributes, it ended up having some of the features of both systems, or state capitalism. While state capitalism is not new, it has generated new momentum in recent years. Since the 2008-2009 global financial crisis, Chinese officials have increasingly become skeptical about Western free-market capitalism. Given the tight connection between government and business, China has naturally and increasingly practiced state capitalism. About 80 percent of Chinese companies on China's stock market are backed by the state. The Chinese government may not be familiar with the term "state capitalism," but they no doubt believe that, by incorporating the "visible" hand of government with the "invisible" hand of the market, it can provide stability as well as growth.

As Ian Bremmer predicts, the state capitalism model is on the rise to compete with the free-market capitalism model. The problem of state capitalism is that when the government favors large state-owned companies, small and medium sized private firms suffer. In 2009, China Mobile and China National Petroleum Corporation made profits of $33 billion – more than China's 500 most profitable private companies combined.[25] This will inhibit private entrepreneurship in China, which is a major engine of China's economic growth. Another problem of state capitalism is that state officials make arbitrary decisions that affect the global market. But for now, state capitalism has its appeal for China.

It gives Chinese state companies the clout that private companies in free market economies would take years to build – however unfair it may be. And it helps China make its mark on the world.

Rampant Corruption

In the West, governments are often considered a nuisance and are associated with inefficiency. Many vital functions of society are performed by private enterprises, nonprofit organizations, and religious groups. In China, the government is like a jack-of-all-trades and has its hands "dirty" in everybody's business. This is one of the reasons for rampant corruption in China. According to China's top prosecutorial office, over the past three decades thousands of officials have fled overseas with as much as $50 billion in stolen government funds.[26] With the aid of overseas criminal gangs, those former officials laundered money, obtained fake IDs, and bought real estate in foreign countries.

Endless scandals such as counterfeit drugs, tainted milk powder, and poisoned pet food sparked widespread international fear about the safety of Chinese products. In 2007, the Chinese superior court sentenced the former head of China's State Food and Drug Administration, Zheng Xiaoyu, to death for taking $850,000 in gifts and bribes linked to substandard medicines that caused several deaths.[27] Zheng was one of the highest officials put to death for corruption. People told me, however, that Zheng's sentence was more symbolic, rather than an act of justice. "It is trying to show that the central government had a grip on corruption," a friend said to me. "Many people who had taken much bigger bribes got away. It was like 'to kill a chicken in order to warn the monkeys.' "[28]

However, the situation hasn't improved much. The "monkeys" just get smarter. In China's flashy shopping malls, you will often see two men shopping together. If you were to think they were a homosexual couple, you would be mistaken. They are a different kind of couple, public and private. One is the public official and the other the private businessman. It is the official who does the shopping and the businessman who does the paying. In most cases, a businessperson coordinates with an official's staff to set up accounts at some luxury stores. The official or his family members need only give the account number and pass code at stores, and the purchases are charged to that account. No one even knows who has bribed whom.

Today, there may be a Chinese dream to make a fortune, but there is no Chinese dream to achieve greatness. Many of my friends doing business in China complained about under-the-table deals, but many of them also more or less participated in them because bribery is "expected" and has become an accepted practice.

To complicate matters, gift giving and receiving are conventional ways of social interaction. There is no clear distinction between personal and business relationships. Zhang Ning, a friend of mine in Beijing who runs an advertising magazine for hotels and restaurants, said her clients are her friends. She socializes with them after work for dinner and shopping. The concept of conflict of interest does not exist. In fact, it is all about conflict of interest—their businesses depend on whom they have relationships with. Not only do they not mind opacity, sometimes they even prefer it. As a famous Chinese saying says, "If the water is too clean, there will be no fish." And there are a lot of things that are quite fishy.

Unlike in the West, corruption in China occurs more on the local levels. There are many hooligans and local thugs, such as village chiefs and county and city officials, who have no consciences and do not hesitate to abuse power. The higher officials at provincial level or above are usually more decent. Some of them are much disciplined, competent, and have the best interests of the country in mind.

Corruption has become so endemic in Chinese society that it is a national ill. A recent poll by China's state media, Xinhua, shows that corruption remains the number-one issue on the minds of Chinese citizens. Until China has a strong, transparent legal system that follows the rule of law unswervingly, corruption will be like weeds—no matter how much you cut them, they quickly grow back.

The Road Not Taken

The tea in our cups was refilled several times before my conversation with Chen Ling came to an end. Through the hotel lobby window, I could see another sun shower passing through. The rays of golden sunlight shone through the flying clouds. A half-showing and half-hiding rainbow hung low over the mountains.

"What are your dreams for the future?" I asked—a question I always asked when talking to people in China.

She lowered her eyes for a few seconds and said, "I am a pragmatic person and not a dreamer."

Of course. I remembered what my dear friend Xu Xin told me twenty years ago. China is not a place for dreamers. Almost half of the people I talked to said they didn't have dreams, or didn't bother to dream, or there was no use to dream since reality and dreams were too far apart. Some were surprised by my question.

"Now I feel an enormous social responsibility," she added, "because several hundred people in my company depend upon me to have better lives."[29]

I must say that I really admire what Chen Ling has done. In the years following the company restructuring, Chen Ling and her partner acquired more facilities, developed new product lines, and hired more employees. When I called her later for follow-up questions, I often found her visiting factories in rural areas and traveling for business on weekends. The last time I called her on her cell phone, she was in Shanghai with her son. They were going to an interview scheduled with an American high school. Chen Ling had told me previously she and her husband planned to send their son to the United States for high school and college. It is commonly believed in China that sending children to the West to study will give them a much better future. It costs between $20,000 and $30,000 a year for boarding school, which Chen Ling apparently had no trouble affording.

As for Lian Su, she was preoccupied with her newfound passion: buying and selling stocks online. After the layoff, she worked as a part-time clerk in a bank before retiring for good. In the last few years, she found herself busier than ever. Like many people, Su knew next to nothing about the stock market, but that did not prevent her from making tons of money, much more than what she made in the state company. Just as Su thought that capitalism had saved her, the stock market crashed in November 2008, and she lost all her money. Luckily, her husband had a job in a state-owned utility company that was doing exceptionally well. Into her mid-fifties, Lian Su dreamed no more. What she hoped was that her son, now in college, would have a better life than hers.

That evening, I took a walk to West Lake. The Precious Stone Pagoda on top of the hill was illuminated with white light like an angel. The Solitary Hill Island in the middle of the lake gleamed under the moonlight with a mystical grace. I could see some swans swimming in between the lotuses under an arch bridge. I finally understood why people say Hangzhou is a "paradise on earth." One really needs to leave the place in order to appreciate its beauty.

While walking along the lake, I pondered about the road I did not take. What if I had stayed in China; would I be like Chen Ling and have inherited "easy equity" from a state company? Probably not. I would not have been promoted in the first place. Not only because I was too "bourgeois"—someone who liked to put on pretty clothes while others still wore Mao suits—but also because I was a nonconformist who did not like to comply with highly restrictive social norms. I was rebellious and felt uncomfortable in a culture where everyone has to be like everyone else. I would not want my worth to be defined by whether I was willing to sweep toilets in order to be recognized as a "good" employee.

No, I could not have been able to survive in a hierarchical state company with many bosses to please and no real work to do.

Maybe I would have "jumped into the sea" like some of my friends and joined the party of those rushing to be rich. I might have made millions, and perhaps even sold my soul to participate in bribery in order to succeed. Then, I couldn't picture myself having endless dinners with foul-mouthed businessmen who loved to make tasteless jokes. I would be disturbed by going to karaoke bars and dancing with someone who did not know how to hold a proper distance with women. I would not find it fulfilling and satisfying.

Most likely I would have been laid off, like Lian Su, and spent the rest of my life worrying about my health insurance and grieving over my lost pensions. Or perhaps I would have put up with an unhappy marriage and grown old and bitter over time. However, one thing I know for certain is that I would never have given up dreaming. And to dream the impossible dream, as I learned early in my life, is not something you do in China.

I love China and always will. China is the country where I was born and grew up, the country where I have blood connections, and the country that has made me who I am. But whenever I am in China, I find that I love America more than ever, because America is the country where I have found my dreams, the country that gives me a new spirit, and the country that has made me more than who I am.

Oneness in Thought: Linear and Nonlinear Thinking

As China privatized its economy, it adopted many business practices of its Western counterparts. However, aspects of China's business landscape are uniquely Chinese. In particular, China has instituted a form of private business that is not quite private, as government permeates the private sector.

The boundary between public and private is obscured and ambiguous. Such ambiguity is the norm in China as it conforms exactly to Chinese thought processes.

As Wu Haitao pointed out, the Western way of thinking is based on logic: cause and effect, from point A to point B—it's characterized by linear reasoning. The Chinese way of thinking, influenced by the Taoist beliefs that events in the world are constantly changing and there is no absolute certainty, is based more on intuition. In another words, it is nonlinear thinking. This kind of thinking is prevalent not only in China, but also in other Asian countries and certainly in the Middle East and Muslim culture.

In the West, clarity is highly valued; something should be either one thing or another, *either* in the private sector *or* in the public sector. In China, things do not have to be either-or, but can be both: *both* in the private sector *and* in the public sector. The Chinese are so used to ambiguity that they don't even see the need to make things clear. This is not to say that the ambiguity is a good thing or necessary. It's just a fact in China. Sometimes, ambiguity is intended to avoid an awkward situation, as in the poem "the sun appears in the east while the rain falls in the west; can you tell me whether it is clear or overcast?" Other times, it is to cover dubious business practices, as in the saying "if the water is too clean, there will be no fish." And even other times, it is to shun individual responsibility.

Both linear and nonlinear ways of thinking have their strengths and weakness, and they are complementary to each other. Linear thinking is highly effective in situations that are concrete, well defined, and analyzable. Examples where this kind of thinking is successful are in areas such as law, science, and engineering. Linear, logical thinking is used in writing and enforcing unambiguous laws, in analyzing the results of a laboratory experiment, and in engineering a bridge design based on accepted engineering formulas. The strengths of linear thinking are logic, clarity, and articulation.

Nonlinear thinking is very effective in situations that are ambiguous, murky, multidimensional, and uncertain. Examples of such domains include art, interpersonal relationships, and business strategy. Nonlinear, intuitive thinking is used in creating a painting, in understanding nuances of human behavior, and in weighing one's strengths and weaknesses against one's competitors to chart the course of a business. The strengths of nonlinear thinking are a greater ease with uncertainty, an acceptance of the unknown, and an understanding that reality is often complicated and multidimensional.

In today's globalized world, it is in our best interest to learn from each other. Once we understand the different modes of thought between the West and East, such as linear versus nonlinear thinking, we can see they are actually complementary, like the right and left sides of the brain. By learning to use both, we can achieve a greater oneness in thought that we can use to enhance personal and global problem solving for the betterment of all.

CHAPTER 2

Collective Identity Crises

"The key to change... is to let go of fear."
– ROSANNE CASH

"Change always comes bearing gifts."
– PRICE PRITCHETT

∽

S ituated on the estuary of the Yangtze River, Shanghai is China's most dazzling city with a population of sixteen million. For the last three decades, Shanghai has become a futuristic international metropolis that commands attention from all over the world. The flamboyant skylines of Pudong, the new district on the east bank of the river, have become the symbol of the new China. On the west side of the river is the financial district, known as The Bund, housing the world's largest banks. The architectural styles of the buildings range from Romanesque to Gothic to Renaissance to Art Deco. Here, Western influence on China could not be any more prominent. Each time I visited Shanghai, I could feel the dynamism of New York City while enjoying the glamour of Paris.

Three decades after it adopted its open-door policy, China has become one of the most open economies in the world. Approximately 70 percent of its GDP comes from international trade. Multinational corporations have made significant inroads into all parts of China. Not only have they brought Western goods to China, but also Western ideas, knowledge, and lifestyles.

Globalization helped create an urban "white collar" middle class in China. Many of them work in thriving private enterprises and multinational corporations. They are significantly younger than their Western counterparts. Most were born after the Cultural Revolution (1966-1976) and grew up in an increasingly prosperous and fast-changing China. Savvy with the Internet and mobile devices, they are dynamic, optimistic, and upwardly mobile. They are also living with extreme anxiety due to the rapid changes in China. They are very proud of what their country has achieved in recent decades. While some have shown nationalistic tendencies, many are becoming increasingly westernized. They tend to be more individualistic than older generations, and care more about the environment and personal well-being, and, in the meantime, struggle to find their own uniqueness in a collective culture.

Here, you will meet several of them.

A New Land of Opportunity

Veronica Chen is one member of the young and upwardly mobile new middle class. She has everything that her parents' generation did not have—a good education, economic freedom, and abundant opportunities. After college, Veronica worked in an executive search firm for six years before she started her own recruiting business. I met her in her new office not far from downtown Shanghai. She wore a white linen outfit with a light sage cashmere sweater, looking agile and career-oriented. As she quickly moved some unpacked boxes, Veronica poured me a cup of tea and sat down with me on a couch next to the door, eager to start the conversation. She was articulate, outgoing, and spoke fluent English.

"There are a lot of opportunities," she said, "China's private enterprises are trying to scale up, and they are experiencing a bottleneck. Since I have been working in this industry for six years, I feel I know quite a lot about the industry. I hope to be able to help them."[30]

At age twenty-nine, Veronica appeared mature and independent. "This is not an easy decision, of course. There are a lot of risks, you know, and a lot of competition. But, I love the freedom of having my own business. I hope to be able to create my own brand."

China has become a new land of opportunity. Many of my Chinese friends are returning to China, and even some of my American friends are going to China because of the tremendous opportunities presented there.

Ying Hui-er, a fund manager in a financial institution in Shanghai, is another young woman who benefited from China's economic boom. Making a salary of 10,000 yuan ($1,500) a month, Ying also had a thriving side business—a boutique fashion shop on eBay China, selling women's clothing that imitates the outfits of Hollywood stars and celebrities. "I follow these stars closely and see the latest styles they wear," she said. "And then I can always find almost exactly identical outfits online at a very reasonable price." Her online business generated four times as much income as the salary from her day job. In the meantime, Ying was contemplating starting an online social networking site for young mothers. "Now, these young mothers like to blog and upload pictures of their babies," Ying said. "I want to create a platform for them to share ideas about raising their children."[31]

Many young people I met told me that they felt they were very fortunate to be living during good times. "My parents' generation had nothing," Veronica said. "They are completely lost."

Knowing that I was writing a book about the Chinese middle class, Veronica showed great interest. "When I first graduated from university," she said, "I wanted to become a journalist. But after internships at different media companies, I realized that there was no way to become a real reporter in China. So, I joined a Hong Kong executive search firm."

"How did you feel about that?" I asked.

"I was very angry before," Veronica said. "That was my original dream! But now, the government has loosened up control, and the level of freedom is much better than before. It is also because there is no way to censor—a lot of news is going onto the Internet. Even if the government cracks down on some sites, people can go through special servers and dynamic IP addresses to look for the truth."

People in the West wonder how the Chinese can tolerate the tight controls on the Internet. For the Chinese, the situation has already improved. For example, people now can criticize the government on the Internet as long as they do not organize large-scale antigovernment movements. This would have been impossible ten years earlier. Even some of my American friends told me that when they first went to China, they were angry that some sites such as Wikipedia and Facebook were being blocked. After a while, they became used to it and found ways to work around it. Keep in mind that the Chinese people have never had the freedom of a full flow of information, so they might not know what they are missing.

Although some foreign social media websites are blocked, China has its own version of social media sites. Weibo, a combination of Facebook and Twitter, was launched in August 2009, and has grown into a monster with more than 300 million users by 2012. People post just about everything on Weibo, from celebrity news to fashion snapshots to social debates. The government still tries hard to control Weibo and other media outlets online by blocking key words. However, the Internet has become a new platform for the Chinese people to express their views and opinions.

"Most people don't care about politics now," Veronica said. "They only care about having a good life, being trendy and fashionable."

Veronica Chen has also given up her dream to be a reporter. For now, she wants to focus on her business. "Being an entrepreneur gives me a big heart," she said. "Now, my dream is to realize my full potential, and I feel I can do so through my business." After a pause, she added, "My secret dream is to build a house on the bank of beautiful Er Hai (a lake in Yunnan province in southern China) and spend the rest of my life there."

My American Dream

It is refreshing to hear that, in today's China, young people are talking about their dreams and the freedom of having their own businesses. When I left China twenty years ago, there was no Chinese Dream. I had to leave my country and come to America to pursue my dream of a better future.

In January 1989, I arrived in the United States with two suitcases full of my favorite books and pretty clothes, and started my graduate study at Southern University of New Hampshire (SUNH). My scholarship included a work-study program, which required me to work twenty hours per week on campus. I did not know a soul in America. Fortunately, the university arranged for my accommodations. I lived off campus in a big house shared with twenty-three other young women. It was nicely furnished, with a beautiful living room, a library, and a large kitchen. Some of the women living there were international students like me. A housemother, Ruth, lived with us as a manager. Every Sunday, there was freshly baked bread for us to enjoy with breakfast. A church or YMCA must have sponsored the house, since rent was very affordable. I had a small room with a bed and a chest, and shared the bathroom with a few other girls. All seemed unthinkable luxuries in China.

I soon learned that my English vocabulary was limited. I remember asking one of the girls upon my first arrival: "Where is the water closet?" holding my fingers to show the sign of WC.

She gave me a kind of look that made me feel that I was from another planet. "Oh, you mean bathroom? It's over there." I stared at her with my mouth open: Isn't the "bathroom" supposed to be a place where you take a bath?

In a way, I *was* from another planet. I did not even know who Michael Jackson was. Many things I knew about America came from listening to Voice of America. I was blown away when I learned that Americans threw eggs at their president. Such things were beyond my frame of reference. First, the president—the head of a country—was unquestionably revered in China. People worshiped Mao like worshiping a god. Many would bow to him as if bowing to an emperor. Second, when I grew up, many food products such as eggs and meats were rationed. We rarely had eggs in our meals. The only time I ate eggs was when I was ill. My mother believed the nutrition in eggs could help boost my immune system. I remember seeing her using her fingers to get the last drop of egg white from the eggshell. You do not just throw such precious eggs away, let alone throw them at the president of the United States of America.

My first few years in America were overwhelming, to say the least. I was stressed by the sounds of cars on the highways, horrified at the prospect of giving a class presentation, and confused at the supermarket when the clerk asked, "Do you want a paper or plastic bag?"—as I was not used to having choices. There were so many things for me to absorb, to learn, and to adjust to. Perhaps one of the most titillating events of my early days in America is that I was visited by the FBI.

It was February of 1989. A couple of weeks after I arrived, a stern man in his early fifties showed up at the front door of the house and asked to see me. He was slightly bald and wore a long coat. He introduced himself as an FBI agent and wanted to "have a chat" with me. My first reaction was "Does FBI stand for something else?" Since "bathroom" could mean "water closet," FBI could very well mean something other than *FBI*.

"Do you know about the FBI?" he asked, seeing that I was not particularly surprised. "It's the Federal Bureau of Investigation."

I nodded my head, *the FBI.* He immediately assured me, "Don't worry. This is just a routine checkup. I am going to ask you a few questions."

I was not worried because I knew for certain that I did not do anything that would invite an FBI investigation. In fact, I was more thrilled than anything else. I thought the FBI only existed in movies. Even in my wildest dreams, I would not expect an FBI agent to pay me a visit.

He asked me some questions, such as what I planned to do in America and whether I was a member of the Communist Party. That was easy. I wanted to come to America, and I was never a member of the Communist Party. In the half hour of our meeting, I probably asked him more questions than he asked me. "Why did Americans burn their flag?" I asked, as I had just seen it on TV. "Is that considered unpatriotic?" "Do Americans *really* throw eggs at their president? In China, they would be killed immediately." I went on and on.

"Well, this is a free country," he said, amused by my questions. "Welcome to America."

I felt exuberant, like a bird out of a cage yearning for adventure in the limitless sky. My first American experience was to work as a waitress to help support myself while earning my master's degree. Some of my fellow Chinese students considered it embarrassing to be waiters or waitresses. "Had we not come to the United States," some lamented, "we would have held high positions in government." Coming from a country where no one had to look for work, they found it hard to adjust. But I enjoyed running around the restaurant with a large tray of food, smiling and sweating. It was so American! Something about the experience was very satisfying. That was the beginning of my American Dream.

I often ponder how the events in the world shape our lives. I was on a visa that required me to return to China after I got my degree. However, a few months after I arrived in the United States, the Chinese students protested in Tiananmen Square, demanding more democracy. They erected a "Statue of Democracy," which was modeled after the Statue of Liberty. The demonstration lasted more than a month and captured the hearts of people around the world. I watched the entire event unfolding on television. Like other Chinese students in the United States, I protested with them on the streets. We were furious when we saw the armed tanks raiding the streets of Beijing. We marveled when we saw a courageous Chinese student standing in front of the tanks, using his body to block them from marching into Tiananmen Square. After the crackdown, many of us felt an unspeakable sense of despair. We were fearful about any prospect of returning to our own country. In order to protect the Chinese students from persecution, President George H. W. Bush issued an executive order to grant green cards to all the Chinese students in the United States. This changed my life forever.

As soon as I finished my studies at SUNH, I went to California for an employment opportunity. At the farewell party in our house, one of the girls asked me, "Are you scared of going to California?"

"Scared?" I said. "I can't wait to go."

Nationalism and Westernization

Ironically, nineteen years later, during the torch relay for the 2008 Beijing Olympics, Chinese students both inside and outside the country protested against the opposite side—the West. They stood behind their government, protesting against Western media's reportage on Tibetan unrest. When the "holy flame" of the Olympic torch was extinguished several times during the short relay that ran through Paris, they became outraged. Thousands demonstrated in front of Chinese outlets of the French supermarket chain Carrefour. Some of China's "angry youths" called for a boycott of French products. Jin Rao, a twenty-three-year-old young man, set up an "anti-CNN" Web site to rebut Western media reports about China. Countless short videos with strong nationalistic rhetoric were posted on YouTube.com and received millions of views.

Because of China's phenomenal growth in recent decades, many young Chinese feel tremendous pride for what their country has achieved. Some told me that the arrogance of American-centric rhetoric in Western media annoyed them. "I feel that the Chinese government has no status (reputation) on the international stage," Veronica said. "But it's unfair that Western media demonize China." Richard Chen, a bright student in Zhongshan University in Guangzhou and an admirer of America, told me that he suspected the West was conspiring to irritate the Chinese government and blemish the Beijing Olympics. Some even believed that talk of democracy and freedom of speech were deceptive tricks used by the West to push its agenda.

However, I believe that the nationalistic rhetoric by China's "angry youth" is reactive rather than proactive. The Chinese still remember that the West treated China poorly about a hundred years ago. In the nineteenth century, Western powers such as the United Kingdom and France expanded their colonies and sought overseas markets for their goods. In 1839, the United Kingdom declared war on China, known as the First Opium War, to force China to allow free trade. Under military coercion, China signed the Treaty of Nanking, which the Chinese consider as an unequal treaty. China paid the British an indemnity, ceded the territory of Hong Kong, and agreed to establish a "fair and reasonable" tariff. It was followed by the Second Opium War with Britain (1856-1860), the Sino-French War (1884-1885) over territorial control of Tonkin (northern Vietnam), and the Sino-Japan War (1894-1895) over control of Korea. All ended with defeats for China. The Chinese consider this part of history to be very humiliating.

That is why many Chinese still have a defensive attitude towards the West.

In 2009, the Brookings Institution held a special panel discussion, "Understanding China's "Angry Youth": What Does the Future Hold?"[32] Among the distinguished panelists were Kai-Fu Lee, then president of Google China, Evan Osnos, the *New Yorker* staff writer who authored an article titled "Angry Youth," academics, and other China experts. The panelists believed that much of the concern about China's nationalism is overblown. As Kai-fu Lee pointed out, the so-called "angry youths" are not the majority, and "certainly not the ones showing true leadership."

On the contrary, Chinese young people are becoming increasingly westernized. In the United States, the discussion about globalization is often about the jobs outsourced to overseas and how America is losing its competitive advantage. Yet when I travel in China, it is very apparent to me that a major part of globalization is westernization, or more specifically, Americanization.

The Starbucks at Metro City in west Shanghai was probably the busiest Starbucks I visited in China. Situated inside a gigantic glass ball, a distinguished landmark of the area, newly minted coffee drinkers packed the place. Most of them worked in the surrounding office buildings that housed multinationals like Microsoft and Softbank. Although spacious, it felt cramped with a roomful of young men and women sipping lattes and tapping on laptops. This could be any Starbucks you would find in the United States: a stunningly inviting interior, espresso aroma filling the air, and the unmistakable music of Elvis Costello. Only one thing was startlingly different: the clientele was much younger—almost all of them were in their twenties and thirties.

I was there to meet a blogger, Wang Jianshuo, who worked in an Internet company. Wang's blog had attracted attention from Western media such as BBC and NBC. Born in 1977 to a family of intellectuals in a third-tier city in Henan province, Wang came to Shanghai at age eighteen to attend Jiao-tong University.

After college, he worked as a software engineer, first at Microsoft Development Center in Shanghai, and then at Kijiji, eBay's classified ads business in China. In his own words, he enjoyed "pure geek happiness" at work. He has a typical happy-go-lucky personality. A fan of Jack Welch, former chairman and CEO of General Electric, Wang was well read and well informed about the outside world. Sipping espressos in an American café, working for an American company, studying American business icons, and blogging to an audience that includes major American media, this young man demonstrates how globalization has brought America to the Chinese middle class.

Wang Jianshuo is not an unusual example. Westernization seems to be everywhere in China. Many young Chinese I met adopt English names and pride themselves on being westernized. Pirated versions of TV shows such as *Friends* and *Sex and the City* are very popular in China. Kentucky Fried Chicken (KFC) has become the favorite meal for Chinese youth and children. I know that the best treat for my seven-year-old niece in China is to take her out to the local KFC. Coca-Cola drinks have found their way into remote villages.

Jenny Chen, a young woman who was vice president of BlogBus, an Internet start-up company, proudly showed me her office, where a model of Capitol Hill—not the Forbidden City—stood on her desk. Bill Gates is much more a hero among Chinese youth than he is in the United States. Young people celebrate Christmas more than Chinese New Year—not because they are Christians, but because Christmas is a Western tradition, considered modern and trendy in China.

An additional aspect of westernization is that Chinese society has also become more pluralized. In Guangzhou, I was surprised to meet a gay man, Curtis Chin, who openly declared his homosexual orientation without hesitation. According to Curtis, approximately one hundred million people, or 8 percent of China's population, are homosexual. Official government data identifies

3 percent of Chinese as homosexual. "People are more open-minded now," Curtis said. "Although some people still hide their sexual orientation, more and more people have begun to accept the idea."

Curtis' parents were former Red Guards. "My parents told me some interesting things about the Cultural Revolution," he said. "They traveled all over the country on free trains, and they went to Beijing to see Chairman Mao." Yet Curtis felt drawn by Western culture. He had traveled to many parts of Europe. "I visited five countries in Europe—Ireland, Switzerland, Belgium, Denmark, and France—in one trip," he said. "I stayed in youth hostels, sharing a room with eight or twelve people—mixed with men and women. It was a lot of fun. When I was in Europe, I did not feel any culture shock. People are open to new ideas and concepts."

Living with a boyfriend, Curtis dined out three or four times a week with friends and hung out in bars on weekends. "My generation (thirty years old) wants to think for ourselves and speak for ourselves," he said. "My parents were brought up to believe in sacrificing for the country. But I want to focus on my life."[33]

As I was talking to Curtis, all the dramatic events that have made up China's recent history, such as the Cultural Revolution and the Tiananmen Square democratic demonstrations, seemed too remote from the reality of today's China.

Extreme Optimism and Anxiety

There is a surging optimism among the Chinese people today that I have never seen before. A Pew Global Attitudes Survey indicates that more than two-thirds of Chinese expect their personal position to improve in the coming years.[34] In the meantime, the Chinese are also living with extreme anxiety. They observe that some people suddenly become rich, while others remain poor. They are worried about being left behind.

Liu Xueshan, a civil engineer in Chongqing, felt astounded by his good fortune but also stressed by modern China's fast-paced lifestyle. Born in Qingdao, Shandong province, Liu went to Qing Hai, a province in western China, with his grandparents in the early 1970s. He attended Chongqing University and studied civil engineering. Graduating in 2002, Liu started working for an engineering design firm in Chongqing.

Liu felt very lucky to get this job. He earned a salary of 15,000 yuan ($2,100) a month after taxes, which was considered a good income for a second-tier city like Chongqing, where the cost of living is lower than Beijing and Shanghai. His firm grew very quickly, from about ten to more than 150 employees in less than ten years. Liu worked on many big bridge projects, including bridges on the Yangtze River and the Pearl River in Guangzhou.

"I couldn't believe my luck," Liu said. "I was worried that I was not skillful enough. So, I worked very hard. Often, I had to stay overnight to get my work done. Many of us work countless sleepless nights before deadlines. It's very challenging and stressful, because many of our projects are high profile and receive a lot of attention from the public and the government."[35]

China has constructed substantial infrastructure in recent years. Because China developed so rapidly, many construction projects had to finish very quickly. Hangzhou Bay Bridge, a twenty-two-mile-long bridge across the sea that cost $2 billion to build, took only five years to complete. "Can you imagine it?" Liu said. "The same kind of project would take at least ten years in the United States, right? And here, right where we are standing (his office building) was farmland three years ago. Look at all the buildings and development here! New cities are emerging like bamboo shoots after the spring rain. Can you imagine it?"

Liu and his wife bought a two-bedroom apartment when he graduated from college. "Now that we have a baby, the apartment is too small for us," he said. "Our parents moved here to live with us and help us. We like that."

They had just acquired a larger four-bedroom apartment and were still in the middle of constructing the interior. In China, apartments are sold in shells. Buyers have to do the entire interior, such as floors, walls, ceilings, and so on. "The first apartment was not very expensive," Liu said. "We have almost paid off the mortgage. Now we have a second mortgage for the new apartment."

Like their counterparts in Western countries, white-collar workers in China are under tremendous pressure. "I work six days a week," Liu said. "I don't have much free time. Work takes up much of my time. I often have to work in the evenings, especially when there is a deadline. And we spend a lot of time dining with customers. I hardly have any time to have dinner with my family. Even though I earn a good income, I don't have time to enjoy life." Liu was also concerned about his job security. "Now college graduates cannot find jobs. I think in the future that it is going to be very difficult to find a job. Life is far from easy."

China is in the midst of rapid changes. Many people have experienced tremendous stress and anxiety. Wang Jianshuo, the blogger I met at Starbucks in Shanghai, told me that many of his friends felt that if they were not millionaires within three years after college, they were losers. "Nowadays, being poor is not only being materially deprived, but also spiritually humiliated."

The youth suicide rate is increasing in China. According to the World Health Organization, China's national suicide rate is fourteen per one hundred thousand—high by international standards.[36] Between January and June 2010, twelve workers at Foxconn Technology in Shenzhen jumped off a campus building and committed suicide. Foxconn Technology makes products for the global companies Apple, Dell, and Hewlett-Packard and employs over four hundred thousand workers, most of them rural migrant workers aged eighteen to twenty-four.

Stress and anxiety have already taken a toll on people's mental health. In early 2010, several of China's coastal cities reported mass stabbings of schoolchildren, apparently by people who suffered from mental problems. Mental illness remains a taboo in modern China. There is no sufficient psychiatric treatment. According to the British journal *The Lancet*, an estimated 91 percent of the 173 million Chinese adults who suffer from mental problems never receive professional help.[37]

As a friend of mine told me, the best way to observe the psychology of middle class Chinese was to watch how people catch the bus. You would see people pushing, yelling, and nudging each other in their rush to get on the bus. "Because there are not enough buses," he said, "and the buses do not have enough seats."

China's Inadequate Health Care System

A major cause of stress on the Chinese middle class is China's inadequate health care system.

Before the economic reforms, health care was essentially free in China. In urban areas, state-owned enterprises usually covered at least 90 percent of medical expenses for their employees. In rural areas, peasants also had basic medical treatment at minimal expense.

The economic reforms abandoned the old socialist "cradle-to-grave" welfare system. In the 1980s, China switched to a "market-oriented" health care system. The government dramatically reduced funding for health care, although a new and effective social safety net was not yet in place. Hospitals began to focus on the bottom line rather than providing quality medical care. Many doctors were under pressure to prescribe highly profitable drugs. InMedica, a medical market research firm, estimated that about 53 percent of public hospitals' revenues in 2007 was from the sale of expensive drugs.[38] In many cases, the profits generated from selling drugs accounted for as much as 90 percent of a hospital's income.[39] Doctors also charged steep fees or took bribes for seeing patients and performing operations.

Soaring fees made medical services less affordable to ordinary people. Many people do not have health insurance. According to a 2006 survey by the World Health Organization, nearly 50 percent of health care costs were borne by individuals, 33 percent by various types of insurance, and only 18 percent by the government.[40]

Countless people went broke because of mounting medical bills. China's state media reported that a young man from Xi'an in western China suffered serious spinal injuries in an accident. The cost of emergency room treatment and surgery cost him as much as 100,000 yuan, or $14,700. His family went broke and deeply into debt in order to save him from permanent paralysis. Some people simply have to forgo treatment.

The inadequate social safety net has put a large strain on the fledgling new middle class. Many began to save a significant amount of their income to self-insure for medical expenses. Victor Ku, a hotel manager in Guangzhou, told me that he saved two-thirds of his income. "I have to pay for my own health care expenses," he said. "In China, we don't have security. If you get sick, you can immediately become poor. The government is not going to take care of us any longer. So we need to save to take care of ourselves."[41]

Recently, more and more Chinese middle class families are immigrating to the United States. They saved up enough cash, sent their children to American universities, and bought properties in the U.S. and settled down here. Many told me the main reason for middle class Chinese to immigrate to the U.S. is lack of security. Fundamentally, they don't trust that the Chinese system will protect them and provide the kind of security they need.

In 2009, the Chinese government announced a plan to spend $124 billion to overhaul the country's broken health care system. The goal was to extend medical insurance to 90 percent of population and make "basic health care service" available to all people. The plan set up a blueprint to expand the network of public hospitals, clinics, and community health care centers, making medical services more accessible to average people. Other highlights of the plan include more government funding for hospitals, regulations on prescription drugs, and disease prevention and disease control.

Of the $124 billion investment in health care reform, 50 percent of the funding will be used to expand the coverage of medical insurance, 30 percent for the construction of rural health care facilities, and 20 percent to fund public hospitals, according to InMedica, the England-based medical market research firm.[42]

It is still too early to tell how successful China's health care reform will be. However, it is a step in the right direction. China will need to have a well-established social welfare system to ensure a stable and large middle class.

The Struggle of Individuals in a Collectivist Culture

Traditionally, Chinese culture puts collective interests above individual interests. Many Chinese people I talked to often associated their own future with the future of the country. Their dreams have always connected to a larger identity—*Guoqiang Minfu*, or a strong country and prosperous people.

As blogger Wang Jianshuo told the *Wall Street Journal* during the controversial 2008 Olympic relays, the Chinese people believe national unity is more important, whereas people in the West value individual freedom and self-expression. "There is a big gap between the West and China as to which values are more important," Wang said. Unlike Americans, who separate themselves from their government, Chinese still see the government as their collective "face," especially on the international stage. Therefore, when the government was criticized, Chinese people took it personally and believed they, as a group, were being attacked. When the government was humiliated, they felt they were losing face and, therefore, felt humiliated.

Collective culture has its merits. It gives people a sense of mutual support and belonging. As China transitions to a more open and plural society, many young people are struggling to find their own individuality, but few find it easy to be able to follow their own dreams. Since the Chinese put great value on group expectations, they tend to measure their worth from what society expects of them rather than what they want for themselves. Young people are prone to go with the flow and do what their peers consider "cool." They are under enormous peer pressure in almost every aspect of their life—marriage, career choice, consumption preferences. They feel like they have to "keep up with the Joneses."

Eddie Liu, a software engineer in Microsoft Shanghai, was frustrated about his career path. After graduating from Fudan University, one of the top universities in China, Eddie got a job at Microsoft Shanghai Development Center. He was one of thirty people who Microsoft selected from three thousand applicants. "That was in the years when the Internet had just started," he said. "Studying computer science was considered the coolest thing."

After working at Microsoft Shanghai for two years, Eddie found himself in the wrong profession. He did not like being an engineer anymore. "Now young people want to do hot jobs," he said. "People want to get into finance, logistics, energy, and communications. IT (information technology) is a little bit like yesterday's fashion."[43]

A brilliant young man, Eddie was a natural entrepreneur. He came from a poor family in Fujian, a southern province in China. As a child, he learned to make money by selling T-shirts. "I received 1 yuan ($0.15) for each shirt I sold," Eddie said. "One day, I sold four hundred T-shirts!" He went on to tell me his wildest dream: "China produces about 50 percent of the world's pork," he said. "I want to start a farm to raise pigs and market the pork as a healthy and trendy food." I could easily imagine him to be a Bill Gates or Steve Jobs if he had been born in America. However, the last time I checked his Facebook profile, Eddie was still with Microsoft

Shanghai. In many people's minds, working at Microsoft is probably the best job one could hope for. Yet Eddie Liu felt trapped.

I met a couple on a cruise ship on the Yangtze River. The husband, Wu Xiaoguang, was a researcher in a nuclear power research institute in Beijing, and his wife, Zhang Huimei, worked in a women's association. Wu's company sent him to attend a conference in Chongqing. He brought along his newlywed wife, and they took the cruise on their way home. As we enjoyed the beautiful scenery along the Yangtze River, our conversation turned to Beijing's skyrocketing real estate prices.

"Many young people are under peer pressure to buy homes and cars," Wu said, clearly agitated. "Beijing's real estate was bid up because of this. Beijing already has over three million cars. The current road system cannot handle the traffic. Yet every day, more than one thousand new cars are added onto the streets. Some people buy cars not because they need one, but because it's cool."[44]

Wu and Zhang felt torn. "On one hand, we felt compelled to follow the trend—to do whatever others are doing, to buy homes and cars. On the other hand, we wanted to do something we really liked. But we worry that we will be left behind, which is humiliating."

One serious drawback of collective culture is the "mob effect," which is very apparent in Chinese society. During the Cultural Revolution, Chairman Mao said, "You should be concerned about national affairs." Everybody in the country became fanatical about politics. In the beginning of the economic reforms, Deng Xiao Ping said, "To get rich is glorious." Everybody began to chase money. In recent years, some confused party official said: "Communist belief is no different from religions such as Christianity." Everybody in the country started to tell me the same thing.

Another example occurred after the devastating earthquake of 2008, when the Chinese middle class donated a total of $7 billion to help the disaster area rebuild the region. This is a praiseworthy response, except people donated much of the money because of peer pressure. Right after the earthquake, people started to pressure each other to donate money. I happened to be in China during that time, and many people, sometimes strangers, asked me, "Have you donated money to the disaster area? How much have you donated?" Wang Shi, a real estate tycoon, initially donated 2 million yuan ($290,000). The Chinese "netizens," or Internet users, were furious and attacked him on the Internet, citing someone who made less money than he made but donated 10 million yuan ($1.5 million). Pressured to do so, Wang Shi increased his donation to 130 million yuan ($19 million).

Unable to break away from the enormous social pressure, some have become withdrawn. Wu Xiaoguang and Zhang Huimei, the couple I met on the Yangtze River cruise, told me that they dreamed of living in the countryside with natural beauty, like hermit poet Tao Yuan-ming (365 AD-427 AD). "But there is a big gap between the dream and reality. It's no use for us to dream."

Oneness in Culture: The Individual and the Community

Before we had the Internet and mobile phones, we wrote letters. I have kept some of the correspondences that I exchanged with my family. After I first came to America, I sent my parents pre-printed address labels so they did not have to struggle to write my address in English on the envelope. Each time, I would remind them: "Remember to put your own address on the upper left corner and put my address on the lower right corner of the envelope. This is the American way."

Indeed, it is the opposite way from how Chinese address an envelope. They write the destination address in the upper left corner, and the sender's return address in the lower right corner. Even the order of writing an address is the opposite. In China, it starts with the country, then the province (state), the city, the street address, and finally the recipient's name. In America, the name goes first, then the street address, the city, the state, and finally the country.

Another notable example is the order of a person's first name and last name. Chinese put the family name first; the focus is on the family and ancestors. Americans put their given names first and family names last; the focus is on distinguishing the individual from the family. With a culture that is less hierarchical, some even choose their last names.

While these differences seem trivial, it reflects cultural differences between East and West. Chinese culture values collective effort, believing the national interests are more important than individuals'. In China, individuality is associated with selfishness and carries some negative connotation. Western cultures, on the other hand, applaud personal effort rather than collective endeavor. A critical characteristic of American society is that it encourages personal aspirations and provides the means for people to pursue them. Success depends more on merit than on privilege.

Chinese culture is heavily influenced by Buddhism and Taoism, which stress the individual as part of the whole. This is evident in Chinese traditional brush paintings, where landscape paintings of nature dominate. Individuals are small dots in those paintings and almost invisible. Western culture, influenced by Greco-Roman, classical and Renaissance culture, seems to focus more on the individuals that make up the whole. Western art and sculpture typically focus on the human form.

The East and West are like the yin and yang of the universe. Chinese culture places more emphasis on the feminine energy of the universe (yin), which includes humbleness, patience, letting-be, and motionlessness. Western culture accents the masculine energy of the universe (yang), such as proactiveness, aggressiveness, goal orientation, and taking action. They are two sides of one coin.

Both individualism and collectiveness have their positive attributes. For example, individualism encourages creativity, liberty, and diversity; collectiveness gives people a sense of belonging, and a sense of the community and their relationship within it. In China, collective identity may overshadow individual voices and their uniqueness. In the West, on the other hand, a strong tendency toward individualism often results in self-centered attitudes and lack of collective coherence. The challenge is to balance the two. When people from the East and West learn from each other, we can both become stronger, because both individualism and collectiveness play important roles in our lives and society. We need both to be one.

CHAPTER 3

The Greatest Migration

"Man strives upstream, as water flows downstream."

- CHINESE PROVERB

ᕼᕽ

Today, China is the best place to witness an unprecedented urbanization. In the past two decades, hundreds of millions of people left their rural homes in poor inland provinces and flocked to coastal urban areas looking for jobs and opportunities. China's urban population has more than doubled, growing from 254 million in 1990 to more than 680 million at the end of 2011. More than half of China's population now dwells in urban areas.[45] Over the next twenty years, some 350 million people will move from rural to urban areas, making an urban population of almost one billion.[46]

Probably no other place on earth better epitomizes the pioneering spirit. As I traveled the country, I saw new cities erected on bare land in the middle of nowhere. Small towns grew into large metropolises. Bridges, ports, and railways rose like never before. Since 1990, China has paved 1.5 million miles of new highway, not including reconstructed highway or expressway. That is five hundred times the distance between New York and Los Angeles. In the next twenty years, China will build fifty thousand new skyscrapers, the equivalent of ten New York Cities.[47]

Since 2006, GDP growth in the second- and third-tier cities in China has surpassed that of first-tier cities. The city "tier system" in China is based on population and average income. The four first-tier cities, which have the largest population, highest income and largest GDP, are Beijing (seventeen million people), Shanghai (sixteen million people), Guangzhou (twelve million people), and Shenzhen (ten million people). There are thirty-six second-tier cities that have large populations but rank secondary in income, and some six hundred third-tier cities ranked lower in income. In 2005, about 136 third-tier cities had more than one million people. It is predicted that by 2025, China will have 221 cities with more than one million people, and approximately four hundred million Chinese middle class will live in the second- and third-tier cities.[48]

Unlike farmers in the West, China's peasants were impoverished and underprivileged. Before the economic reform, rural residents could not move to cities. China implemented the household registration system (*hukou*) in the 1950s as an instrument of the planned economy to regulate labor and ensure an adequate food supply for the nonagricultural population. The system ties the state-provided social benefits such as education, medical care, and pension to a person's birthplace. If a person was born in a rural area, he or she would not be able to go to school or find a job in a city. It seriously limited people's mobility. A rural *hukou* could mean a lifetime of hard labor and poverty, in contrast to the stable income, better education, and social benefits available in the cities.

As the reform accelerated, urban income increased dramatically while rural income stagnated, further widening the gap between rural and urban China. In 1984, the government first lifted restrictions, allowing peasants to leave their farmlands and go to cities to seek employment opportunities.[49] Since then, wave after wave of young rural men and women, referred to as "migrants" or "migrant workers," have been constantly on the move to coastal urban areas each year in search of better lives.

Work Hard and Get Ahead

Here come the sons and daughters of peasants, who are no longer satisfied with being tied to the land. They come because they have seen their parents and grandparents struggle hopelessly in a vicious cycle of poverty. They come, with their relatives, friends, and fellow villagers, to the cities where life seems as promising as the skyscrapers. They come with nothing in their possession but a blanket roll to keep warm at night and some clothes to hold their dignity during the day. They come with no skills whatsoever, but the willingness to work hard and the determination to change their destiny. They come by the hundreds of millions with great expectations that they will find jobs, they will make money, and they will live better lives.

Yi Fan is one of them. He not only pulled himself up out of poverty but also helped his family. Born in 1975, Yi Fan is the third child in an impoverished peasant family. Like other peasants in China, his parents worked in the fields growing crops. Yi Fan and his siblings began to help in the fields at a very young age. "By the end of the year," Yi said, "all the crops were delivered to the government, and very little was left over for ourselves." The main source of income was from his mother, who raised pigs to sell in the market. They lived in a shabby abode with a straw roof and mud walls. Yi Fan grew up never having clothing that was not patched. Although his father wanted to send his children to school, the family was so poor that they could not even afford to pay the eight yuan ($1) tuition fee. Life was nothing but misery and hardship.

Even in urban areas, living standards were very marginal compared to Western standards. When I grew up, my family lived in a three-story building that looked very much like a high school building in the United States. It had a hallway in the middle and individual rooms on both sides. There were no kitchens. Residents cooked in the hallway with their coal stoves, making the entire hallway pitch-black like a coalmine. We shared toilets and sinks, which were usually not in a very sanitary condition. Yet it was a good neighborhood since the people who lived there mostly worked for the provincial government. I suppose "poverty" is a relative term. We were much better off compared to rural people even though we lived with minimal material means.

Although a child stricken by poverty, Yi Fan was not lacking in imagination. While laboring in the fields, he always looked at the mountains surrounding the village and wondered what was beyond them. "My childhood dream was to see the outside world," he said. As soon as he turned eighteen, Yi Fan joined the tide of migrant workers and headed to Guangdong province, a popular destination for rural migrants. He knew there was no future for him in his village and was determined to look for a better life beyond the high mountains.

Many rural migrants from inland provinces such as Hubei, Anhui, and Sichuan rushed into Guangdong, where the manufacturing industry and new private businesses were booming. Many migrants went to work for foreign-owned factories or joint ventures that produced toys, garments, electronics, and other consumer goods. Others went into construction to build highways and high-rises to modernize China. Many others found their way into retail stores and restaurants that were mushrooming all over the area.

With the help of his uncle, who was a migrant worker himself, the young Yi Fan got his first job in a factory that produced plastic flowers. The factory provided free room and board. He lived in a dormitory where he shared a 400-square-foot room crammed with twenty-three other people. All of them were rural migrants from different provinces. "The food was terrible," Yi said. "But I made 300 yuan ($36 a month)!" That was a lot of money for him. He knew that it would take a full year's hard work for his parents to earn that much. Consequently, Yi Fan sent all the money he earned back home.

While working in the factory, Yi Fan kept his eyes open for other opportunities in this booming metropolis. A few months later, he saw a newspaper ad for a waiter in a local seafood restaurant, Shao Er Zai. He went for the interview and got the job. From then on, the wind was blowing at his back and the sun was shining on his face. He started as a waiter earning 500 yuan ($60) a month and worked his way up to become the manager, supervising a staff of 150 employees. That was the beginning of Yi Fan's Chinese dream.

Restaurants in China can seem grandiose to many Westerners. In the United States, I have never seen a restaurant that has more than one hundred tables. However, in China, many restaurants look like hotels with several floors and hundreds of tables. As China's economy grew at a double-digit rate, the restaurant business seemed to quadruple. In the next three years, Shao Er Zai branched out to many major cities. In the meantime, Yi Fan was promoted to general manger, earning a monthly salary of 10,000 yuan ($1,250).

Within five years, Yi Fan's life had changed, as the Chinese say, like "the sky has flipped and the earth made anew." The money Yi Fan sent back home helped his family improve their living conditions. His parents used the money to build a new house and pay for his younger sibling's schooling and other expenses.

However, Yi Fan realized that in order to get his family completely out of poverty, he would need to find a way to bring them to the city, where life was much better. There was not enough arable land for peasants to make a decent living farming. The income gap between urban and rural areas continued to widen. Yi Fan was glad that at least he had a chance. The reform enabled rural migrants with stable jobs in the cities to register as urban *hukou* (household registration system) and apply for the same status for their immediate family members. Some cities have special policies to favor those who own properties or businesses in the cities where migrant workers intend to stay.

At age twenty-three, Yi Fan began to dream big. He partnered with a friend and started a business selling mobile phones in Guangzhou. It was perfect timing. China was on its way to becoming the largest mobile phone market in the world. If the restaurant business quadrupled, the cell phone business grew tenfold. He and his partner reaped handsome profits by distributing cell phones from manufacturers to retail outlets. Within two years, Yi Fan made a fortune of 3 million yuan ($375,000).

Merely twenty-five, Fan had his first taste of success. He bought a three-bedroom apartment in Guangzhou and treated himself to a Honda sedan. Being a homeowner, Yi Fan obtained a Guangzhou *hukou* and officially became a city resident. It was like an illegal Mexican immigrant being granted a green card in the United States. Yi Fan's next plan was to bring his family to Guangzhou, which he saw as an ultimate solution to escape poverty. "My goal was to make 10 million (yuan) before I reached thirty," he said. "I am glad that I was born poor. I must work very hard, and I will not stop until I reach my goals."[50]

Yi Fan's story should sound familiar. It exemplifies what has made America a great country—the can-do spirit, optimism, and determination to pursue a better life and leave the next generation better off than one's own. Today, many middle class Americans and Westerners are less optimistic and are under tremendous financial and emotional pressures. As they sweat about the uncertainties in their future, perhaps they will be inspired by how the American spirit has influenced people in China and other parts of the world.

My Journey as a New Immigrant

It was that spirit that sustained me through both good and bad times as a new immigrant in America.

As soon as I arrived in California from New Hampshire, I changed my name from Haiyan to Helen. Like many Chinese immigrants in the United States, I wanted to have an English name and desired to fit into the mainstream Western World. Although people told me that my Chinese name, Haiyan, sounded pretty, I felt that it was too Chinese for me. "Haiyan" literally means "sea swallow" in Chinese. Imagine someone calling you: "Hello, Sea Swallow!" It is similar to how I call my parakeet: "Hello, bird!" Secondly, it is a common name in China, which conflicted with my desire to be different and unique. Lastly, it was too "revolutionary" due to its origin in a revolutionary poem.

My father was influenced by Russian writer Maxim Gorky's poem "The Song of the Sea Swallow" (also translated as "The Song of the Storm Petrel"). Gorky wrote it in 1901 as a challenge to the tsar, predicting that a revolution was imminent. It starts with striking imagery in sentences like, "Over the gray plain of the sea the wind gathers storm clouds. Between the clouds and the sea proudly soars the sea swallow, as a streak of black lightning." While other birds trembled and cowered, the poem says, the sea swallow cries out with joy to welcome the storm. "In that cry— the lust of the storm! The power of anger, flame of passion and certainty in victory hear the clouds in that cry." The revolution that Gorky predicted turned out to be the Russian Revolution in 1917, which overthrew the tsar-based monarchy and led to the creation of the Soviet Union. The poem was later referred to as "the battle anthem of the revolution."

I remember when I was a child, my father explained to me that the sea swallow was a brave bird and was not afraid of storms. As I grew older, I started to feel that the name was too childish. Apparently, my father was not the only one who was inspired by the poem. Many Chinese women of my age had the name "Sea Swallow."

The year I came to the United States was indeed stormy. Not only did tanks roll into Tiananmen Square, but also the Berlin Wall fell, which eventually led to the collapse of the Soviet Union and the communist world. I was not political, but I came to think that communism was a big joke. I felt sorry that older generations in China had sincerely devoted their whole life to something that turned out to be not even worthwhile. By dismissing my childish, revolution-attached Chinese name, I wanted to fit completely into the Western world.

The name "Helen" felt suitable as it has the same first letter H, and the story of Helen Keller inspired me. With my new English name, I was determined to become Helen Wang, the American.

In California, you can almost live a perfect American life without knowing English. There are Chinese TV channels, newspapers, grocery stores, travel agencies, and even banks. Many of my friends prefer to stay in the comfort zone of the Chinese community, which is entirely understandable. It is so nice to interact with someone who speaks your language and understands your cultural background. A colleague of mine who speaks fluent English and has lived in the United States for more than fifteen years did not know who the popular TV interviewer Larry King was. She never watched CNN, and she did not need to. Yet I wanted to be as American as I could. I stopped reading Chinese newspapers or magazines, refused to watch Chinese-language TV, and surrounded myself with friends from different ethnic backgrounds. I pushed my limits and forced myself to adapt to mainstream American society.

A couple of years later, I went to Stanford University to get another graduate degree. Since then, I have worked in Silicon Valley technology start-ups, riding the high and low tides of the Internet boom. My story is no different from other Chinese students and immigrants. I struggled and suffered. I fell and picked myself up and tried again. Just as I thought I was on my way to becoming a real American, someone pushed my hot button by asking me my Chinese name.

It was at a social event in Silicon Valley. There was food, wine, and casual conversation. As usual, I introduced myself as "Helen" while mingling with people. One woman looked at me intriguingly and said, "C'mon, what's your real name?" I am sure she meant no harm, but I was offended. After some awkward mumbling, I said something like, "Helen is my real name."

The woman's question, however, made me think about who I really am. I am Chinese by ethnic background, and an American by adoption and citizenship. Sometimes I do not identify myself as either. Despite the fact that I have spent so many years trying to be an American, I still feel I cannot entirely fit into the American mainstream. On the other hand, people in China do not think I am Chinese enough. It is an unsettling feeling when you do not know where you belong. Even more strangely, when I am in China, I feel more like an American, but when I am in America, I feel more like a Chinese. I know I am not alone in this identity crisis. Anyone who has lived in two cultures would feel the same frustration.

It took me years of soul-searching before I realized that whether we are Chinese or American, in essence, we are all one human race, like the leaves of one tree and the waves of one sea. "The earth is but one country and mankind its citizens."[51] Because I have lived at the crossroads of the East and West, it also allows me to transcend some of my limitations and become richer and fuller than I would otherwise have been. I can see that many differences between the East and West are more complementary rather than contradictory. Today, I am not proud of merely loving my countries (by birth or by adoption). Instead, I am proud of loving the whole of humankind.

Being a world citizen, I am not only embracing my Chinese roots and Western culture, but also cherishing the diversity in the world. Years later when I married my husband, who has English and Luxembourgian heritage, I decided to keep my Chinese last name.

"Money Can Buy a House, But Not a Home"

Halfway around the world in China, Yi Fan's life unexpectedly changed, on a train from Guangzhou to Shenzhen.

In January 2000, Yi Fan had only one goal in mind: to make 10 million yuan before he reached thirty. He boarded a train to Shenzhen, hoping to close a few deals before he returned to his hometown for the Spring Festival, the Chinese Lunar New Year. As he waited impatiently for the train to start, Yi Fan reviewed his notes about the customers he planned to visit. Little did he know that what was going to happen on the train would change his life forever.

"Hello," a voice interrupted his thoughts. He looked up and saw a foreigner with a backpack smiling at him. "May I take this seat?" The foreigner pointed to the empty seat next to him.

Yi Fan felt embarrassed because he could not speak English and did not know what to say. Another young man sitting in the opposite seat responded in English, "Sure, please."

For the next forty minutes on the train, Yi Fan watched in awe as the young man conversed with the foreigner in fluent English. He was sad that he could not be part of the conversation. The pain of missing a good education when he was a child hit him hard. He decided that he wanted to catch up in his education. After he got off the train in Shenzhen, he checked into an Internet café and searched for English language schools.

Several years later, I met Yi Fan on the campus of Gateway Language Village (GLV), an English language school on the outskirts of Hangzhou. After that life-changing experience on the train, Yi Fan changed to a different person. Not only did he speak fluent English, he also ran a branch of GLV. Now using an English name, "James," he greeted me with a firm handshake.

"Welcome to GLV," he said in fluent English.

He was a good-looking young man with a Brad Pitt spiky haircut. He wore a pair of blue jeans with a black T-shirt, and was tall and athletic. He was spirited and confident, radiating incredible positive energy.

"I found GLV seven years ago," he said, "and fell in love with it." He first enrolled in GLV as a student, and then decided that he wanted to be part of it. In early 2007 when GLV opened a new branch in Hangzhou, he invested some of his money in the school and became the head of GLV's Hangzhou branch.

Yi Fan had successfully brought his family to Guangzhou. Although *hukou* (household registration system) reform was accelerated in the late 1990s, there were still restrictions on rural migrants obtaining social benefits such as schooling and medical care on an equal basis with city residents. One of the requirements to obtain a city *hukou* was to have a stable income or to own a business. Yi Fan used the money he made from his cell phone business to open two restaurants, and handed them over to his sister to manage daily operations. He also bought a car for his brother to help him become a taxi driver in Guangzhou. With his help, both his brother and sister obtained Guangzhou *hukou* and became urban residents.

In the early years, migrant workers were the major labor resources for foreign-owned and joint venture manufacturers. Over time, they were woven into the whole fabric of urban life—retail stores, restaurants, and private enterprises. Despite the fact that many rural migrants are still at the bottom of society, they feel that they are on their way up. They earn more income than they would otherwise, and have more opportunities for entrepreneurship, which leads to more incomes and better lives.

"GLV was my turning point," Yi Fan said. "I wanted to be rich and become a multimillionaire. Now, I want to be an educator. Making money is easy, but being an educator is something else. Money can buy a house, but not a home."

I was deeply affected by his enthusiasm and optimism. Yet there was something I could not quite put my finger on. In today's highly commercialized China, being rich is not only glorious, but also faddish. I have heard countless stories of the instant rich ostentatiously brandish their wealth. For example, Yi Fan's previous boss Lin Wei-cheng became a multimillionaire by running a seafood restaurant chain. He built himself a five-story mansion with shining glass windows like the office buildings commonly seen in Silicon Valley. In his lavishly ornamented, lobby-like hallway stood two fat Buddha statues plated with 24-karat gold. Colorful tropical fish danced with flashing disco lights in a gigantic fish tank. On his thirty-first birthday, Lin Wei-cheng ordered a five-and-a-half-foot-tall birthday cake and invited newspaper reporters so he could boast of his success.

In this frenzy of chasing after riches, people constantly complain about the moral decay in society. Many business people do not mind crossing an ethical line to lie, cheat, and even kill in order to make more money. I remember reading the horrible news about chemically tainted milk powder sold in Gansu province that killed at least six children, hospitalized 680 babies, and sickened some three hundred thousand more.[52]

Yet here was Yi Fan telling me, "Money can buy a house, but not a home." Why? What inspired him? What made him take a drastically different route from his peers? I was pondering these questions while wandering the corridors of the GLV building. There, on the wall, I found my answer.

A poster on the wall listed the teachers' and staff's names with their pictures. It was a normal poster board like that found in any school, but when I looked at it more closely, I found jewels. Under each name, there was a quote. Here is what they said:

"It is better for a man to lose millions than to lose a good name."

"It is better to light a candle than to complain about the darkness."

"Happiness is not a goal. It is a by-product of living the life of service to others."

"You must be the change you want to see in the world."

Yi Fan had told me how much love these foreign teachers had shared with students and staff. His voice choked with emotion when he spoke. Those Americans, Canadians, and people from other parts of the world came to China to teach English. They brought with them not just English language skills, but a genuine love for China and the Chinese people. This love profoundly touched Yi Fan's heart—it was a love that transcended borders and races, connected strangers, and inspired people to do amazing things.

"I admire education," Yi said. He certainly had his eyes on higher places. "My dream is now to go to America to study for an MBA and become a professional educator." And his next goal? "When I am fifty," he continued, "I will go to the villages to teach rural kids."[53]

Study Hard and Get Ahead

If the American dream is to work hard and get ahead, the Chinese dream is to study hard and get ahead. While the Chinese value working hard, they value education even more. Under the influence of Confucius's teaching that a learned man is a superior man, the Chinese worship education almost to the point of rigidity. An educated person automatically enjoys higher esteem in the society. Many Chinese still scorn peasant upstarts who have little education.

Some rural youths saw education as a route to escape poverty and secure a better life for themselves and their families. With hard work, perseverance, and good luck, some were able to move up and find decent jobs in the city.

Hu Shen-hua was one of those rural youths. His background is similar to Yi Fan's. Born in 1975 to a poor family in rural Hunan province, Hu learned the hardship of life at a very early age. "As a child," he said, "I went into the mountains to chop wood. I was cold and hungry all the time. In the summer, I helped my family work in the fields under the hot sun." Despite all the difficulties,

Hu dreamed of becoming a scientist like Einstein. His parents and grandparents saved every penny to send him to school because they saw it as the only way out for a better life.

In 1992, Hu was one of the few, out of thousands of rural youths, who passed the college exam and went to Beijing Information Technology Institute. For a poor boy like him, going to college is a ticket to city life. After graduation, Hu got his first job at a Japanese joint-venture company doing software quality assurance. From there, he moved on to become a manager at Oracle Software Research and Development Center in Beijing, supervising a team of ten people. Earning a decent salary, he bought a three-bedroom apartment in the outskirts of Beijing. With a stable job, Hu got Beijing *hukou* and officially became an urban resident. He fulfilled his parents' and grandparents' dreams.

Compared to many rural youth, Hu Shen-hua had a better future in front of him. Looking forward, Hu hopes he can give back to his family, who sacrificed a great deal to support him through college. He said, "I am not interested in becoming a billionaire like Bill Gates. But I want to do something to help the poor people in rural areas. They have their dreams too!"[54]

China's Problematic Education System

Their dreams, however, are under threat. For millions of rural youths, the hope of escaping poverty via education is diminishing in the face of intense competition.

The Chinese government provides compulsory education through ninth grade. However, most Chinese schools lack resources and creative teaching methods. Teachers do not make lesson plans. Central or local governmental committees determine textbooks. Teachers come to class and often read directly from these textbooks, and occasionally write on the blackboard. They rarely use visual aids for their classes. In urban areas, children, starting at age six, are buried under an avalanche of studies twelve hours a day without any fun and recreation. In rural areas, schools have a very high student-to-teacher ratio—sometimes over one hundred students per teacher. In addition, most rural schools lack well-qualified teachers and up-to-date course material.

Since the mid-1990s, China has gone through major reforms in its higher education system. New campuses were built on a large scale, and many colleges were upgraded and merged with universities. College enrollments have increased exponentially. In 2007, about twenty-five million students attended China's colleges and universities, compared to merely 6.4 million in 1998.[55]

However, the quality of the education has deteriorated. Many professors spent the bulk of their time making money—charging steep consulting fees to businesses or for private tutoring. Lian Fang, a professor at Zhejiang Art Institute, told me that he charged 100,000 yuan ($15,000) to design packages and advertisements for a company that sold cookies and fruit juice products. Professor Lian's salary was about 7,000 yuan ($1,030) a month. His wife, a music teacher, also made a handsome income by giving private piano lessons.[56] As Harvard mathematician Yau Shing-tung noted, despite the increased levels of funding and much-improved facilities in China's higher-education institutions, the standards of research in China have continued to deteriorate.[57]

Most importantly, China's schools and universities have not adopted a model that encourages creativity and innovation. Students take notes and memorize what teachers and professors say without questioning or independent thinking. As a result, many Chinese college graduates are not well suited for a workplace that requires plenty of individual initiative, critical thinking, and the ability to challenge established authority.

In addition, education has become very expensive. Before 1996, the state provided free college education. Since then, college education has been commercialized. College tuition has soared twenty-five times over the past fifteen years.[58] If living expenses are included, the average cost for a college student is about 40,000 yuan ($5,800) per year. The annual per capita income for rural Chinese, however, is less than 3,000 yuan ($460). Many rural youths simply cannot afford a college education. For those who go to college, the future does not necessarily look any rosier. The massive expansion of college enrollments and the low quality in education have taken the shine off a degree. In recent years, more than one million college graduates have been unable to find jobs, including many with master's degrees and PhDs.[59]

Those lucky enough to find work may have to settle for salaries far lower than what they and their debt-laden parents were counting on. Liu Xueshan, the civil engineer featured in chapter 2, told me that when he graduated from college six years before, it was very easy for him to find a job that paid about 2,000 to 3,000 yuan ($300-$450) per month. Now, college graduates are taking jobs with monthly salaries as low as 1,000 yuan ($150), about the same amount that rural migrants earn without a college education.

The failure of China's education reform has cast a long shadow on the quality of life of the new middle class. Many upper middle class families began to send their children to study overseas, in the hope of securing a better future for them. Since 2008, enrollment of Chinese undergraduate students in U.S. colleges has more than tripled, making them the largest group of foreign students at American campuses. For lower middle class families, their chances for moving up may be hindered. The implications can be manifold. As a Chinese saying says, "It takes ten years to grow a tree, but it takes a hundred years to grow a person."

Myth of China's Manufacturing Prowess

People often compare China's urbanization to Western industrialization in the nineteenth century. In both cases, a large population moved from the country to the city. Society advanced from agricultural to industrial via manufacturing on a massive scale.

However, there is a key misconception about China's manufacturing prowess. The Western Industrial Revolution began with technology innovation, whereas China's urbanization was mainly driven by global demand for manufactured goods and thriving private businesses.

In Europe and the United States, the manufacturing industry was created due to technology innovation. For example, railways came into existence because of the invention of the steam engine; automobiles were created because of technology breakthroughs in automobile engines.

In China, the manufacturing industry is being created in response to global demand. Chinese manufacturers take orders from Western companies that have designed products for their home markets. They are not involved with product development, innovation, market research, or even packaging. Chinese manufacturers have little experience in bringing their own products to overseas markets.

Unlike the manufacturing industry in the West that gave birth to a middle class of both white-collar and blue-collar workers, manufacturers in China mostly absorb surplus labor with few skills from rural areas. Those rural migrant workers live in dormitories, earn very low incomes (about $100 to $200 a month), and hardly fit into the category of the middle class. James Fallows, national correspondent for the *Atlantic*, visited many factories in China. He saw people working on the assembly lines and was convinced that only machines would perform those tasks in the United States.

While people in the West fear China as a global manufacturing powerhouse, the Chinese consider their manufacturers to be the sweatshops for the world and see themselves as being in a disadvantageous position.

Yes, China is making efforts to move up the value chain. The eleventh Five-year Plan (2006-2010) called for "scientific development" and building the country's competitive advantage based on science, technology, and innovation. A key initiative is an increase in the R&D-to-GDP ratio from about 1.3 percent in 2005 to 2.5 percent by 2020.

However, it is highly questionable how much of the funding actually pays for research and development and how well the research transfers into manufacturing. To many local officials, "scientific development" means building empty "industrial parks." For example, during the 2008-2009 global recession, China unveiled *The Ten Industry Revitalization Plan* along with a $586 billion stimulus package to help certain industries become more efficient. Nine percent of the $586 billion stimulus money was explicitly set aside for "industrial upgrading." However, the focus of the plan is to consolidate the steel and auto industries in an effort to eliminate inefficiency. With millions of jobs lost in manufacturing, the government found itself struggling to protect jobs rather than consolidating these industries. Instead, the fund paid to build 176 "high-tech development parks" and 146 "productive technology advancement parks."[60]

Given the unpredictability of the regulatory environment, many Chinese manufacturers tend to focus on short-term gain. They compete on volume and price, cutting corners whenever they can in order to keep the cost down. As a result, some Chinese manufacturers are able to capture a large market share worldwide, but only enjoy wafer-thin profit margins. This has severely hindered Chinese manufacturers from investing in research and development or training employees.

Another big hurdle for China's manufacturers to move up the value chain is lack of a skilled workforce. Many multinationals complained about a shortage of managerial talent. Meanwhile, companies have repeatedly reported that a majority of Chinese workers are inefficient in the workplace. This combination of abundant, low-skilled workers and scarce, high-skilled managerial and technical talent poses a difficulty for Chinese companies to capture more value in manufacturing.

For these reasons, few Chinese companies have ventured outside the country to overseas markets. Those that did positioned their products at the low end for customers in poorer countries such as Africa, and competed on price. Lack of international managerial experience among many Chinese managers is a major obstacle hindering Chinese companies from expanding successfully overseas. For example, strikes and labor conflicts plagued the Shougang Group, China's fourth largest steel company, in its South American ventures.

The root problem is an education system that encourages obedience to hierarchy rather than initiatives and creativity. On one hand, millions of college graduates could not find jobs. On the other hand, companies in need of skilled workers found those college graduates unemployable because of their lack of problem-solving skills. A friend of mine in Beijing who runs a building insulation company told me that migrant workers were more useful than many college graduates were. "At least they are not as picky as the college students," he said.

With college tuition sky high (as much as $15,000-$20,000 for four years), more and more young people turned to vocational schools, which may offer better prospects of employment at lower cost. This means a majority of Chinese workers may be trapped in low-skilled jobs, making China's move up the value chain even more challenging.

While the rest of the world fears China's manufacturing power, China is trying to move away from its "sweatshop" manufacturing and become a service-oriented economy. However, China may find itself locked in a position of being the world's sweatshop for some time because hundreds of millions of rural migrants need jobs.

"Endure the Hardship of Hardships, Become the Man above Men"

When I read the story of a young American woman selling her ova for $7,000 in order to pay off her credit cards, I kept thinking about young women I met in China. They earned about $100 a month, yet saved 80 percent of their incomes to help pay for their siblings' education. I felt a huge disconnection. Although many people are worried that the middle class in the West is shrinking, Americans still enjoy immense privilege compared to the vast majority of people in the world. To many Chinese rural migrants, enduring hardship is their way of life.

On a hot summer day, I was roaming randomly down Jianguomen Avenue in Beijing. I found myself drawn to a place called Liang Zi Fitness. As soon as I stepped in the front door, six young ladies dressed in the traditional Qipao (pronounced chi-pao), a traditional one-piece body-hugging Chinese dress for women, gently bowed and greeted me, "Welcome, distinguished guest."

When I asked what Liang Zi Fitness was, one of the girls politely handed me a menu, which described different kinds of acupressure massages combined with Chinese herbal medicine treatments. Having been cheated in a massage salon before, I was suspicious. However, since I did not have any plans that night, I thought I might as well try it. My favorite massage in China is always the foot massage that is not easy to find in the United States. So, I ordered an "empress foot massage," which cost about $25.

As I was escorted along the hallway, my eyes turned to the grand wall murals that illustrated Chinese ancient mythologies. "This massage place seems a little extravagant," I thought to myself. It was huge: there were two floors with many individual rooms. Along the way, the staff, dressed in traditional Chinese clothes, would stop, bow, and greet me: "Welcome, distinguished guest." "Good evening, distinguished guest."

I was led to a room with a flat panel TV and a couple of massage couches. Before I sat down, a fruit plate and tea were served. Shortly after, my masseur appeared. He introduced himself as "Technician Number 30." He was about twenty years old, attentive and gentle-mannered. His dark skin tone suggested his rural origin (peasants in China usually have darker skin tone because they labor in the field under the sun; light skin tone is considered more desirable in China since it implies the privilege of city life). In our conversation, I learned that he was from Henan province, which is one of the poorest provinces in China and produces the largest number of migrant workers.

He told me the company recruited him and put him through a strict training program. He earned about 3,000-4,000 yuan ($400-$550) per month as a massage technician, with free meals and lodging. The company used a performance-based point system to encourage good customer service and adroit massage skills. That means the more customers who come back to the same massage technician, the more points he or she will earn, and the higher the rate of pay.

I was more than impressed by everything I had experienced so far—the tasteful interior design, the courteous staff, and the excellent service. "Who is the person who started this company?" I asked.

"He was a poor boy from Henan province," he said. "His family was so poor that he never tasted meat before he was ten years old. He started out selling barbecued food on the street when he was thirteen years old. He had done many things, including selling fish, trading clothes, and running a restaurant, before he opened his first foot massage business in Henan. It was 1997 and he was twenty-seven years old. Since then, the business has grown so quickly, and he has opened many branches and made it into a franchise business. Beijing has seven Liang Zi locations, and many want to join the franchise. Now he is rich. He has a big house and two cars."

"What's his name?" I asked.

"His name is Zhu Guofan," he said.

A young girl came in to pour tea in my cup. She wore light makeup, with her hair tied up tidily like a stewardess. Quietly, she retreated backwards as if facing an empress. Just as I was wondering how these young men and women became so well trained and who was responsible, my masseur said, "We have been through military training before we joined the company."

"Military training?" It was as if he had dropped a bomb, and I was immediately alarmed. Having heard so many news stories about hideous abuse to rural migrants, including physical assault and personal humiliation, I was full of sympathy.

"Yes, the company came to our village and recruited us. Then we were all sent to a military compound for one month of military training."

"What did you do at the military training?"

"We got up early in the morning for running and exercising. During the day, we took classes, learning about acupressure points in the human body, and also the company history, corporate culture, and team building."

I was taken aback to hear such things at a foot massage salon. "Corporate culture and team building? Tell me, what is your corporate culture? And what is the team building?"

"Working hard and making progress every day, helping each other and working together to succeed, striving for excellent performance, and providing superior customer service," he said, as if reciting a poem.

"Who paid for all this?"

"The company."

Suddenly, everything made sense to me. China's abundant labor source comes with a cost. Imagine how hard it is to train a large pool of rural people with no job skills. Some entrepreneurs like Zhu Guofan took on the task on their own. In addition to training, the company provides lodging and meals, which saves a lot of trouble for these newcomers as they settle into the cities. No wonder the staff was so warm and professional. No wonder this technician knew the company history by heart. No wonder the tea in my cup never got cold.

"This Zhu Guofan," I said, still in shock. "He was so poor and didn't have much education, right? How did he know about the franchising business and corporate culture?"

"When the business grew so fast, he realized he needed more knowledge in order to keep up with his business. So he enrolled in an eMBA program (an executive MBA program provided for mid-career entrepreneurs). He took a year off to study management."

Technician Number 30 continued, "During Chinese New Year, if we do not go back home, the company throws a big party, and the boss gives each of us a red envelope (it is a Chinese tradition to give New Year's money in a red envelope). The employees here are very happy. Some top performers move up to become managers. They make about 10,000 to 20,000 yuan ($1,470 to $2,940) a month."[61]

"Is that what you plan to do—become a manager?" I asked.

"Maybe," he said. Then he added, "Well, in a few years, I may start my own business. Zhu Guofan encourages us to start our own businesses. He said he would help us. There are many opportunities."

"Is it hard for you, leaving home and working in a big city like Beijing?" I was still probing for some sign of dissatisfaction or bitterness.

He looked at me, with a sparkle in his eyes, and said, "Only if you endure the hardship of hardships will you become the man above men" (a well-known Chinese saying).

I left Liang Zi Fitness late in the night. The lights on Jianguomen Avenue were flickering and shimmering through foggy air, like an abstract painting against dark sky. They were like the sparks I saw in the eyes of Massage Technician Number 30. With those sparks, any adversity or affliction is another stepping-stone to a better life. I have no doubt my masseur will be another Yi Fan, and he will be part of the middle class of tomorrow.

Oneness in Modernization: The Great Rebalancing

During the last several decades, globalization has begot a fundamental economic rebalancing between the developed and developing countries. The centers of economic growth have shifted from developed nations to developing countries. Businesses are seeking opportunities in the emerging markets. Goods, ideas, and knowledge are moving across the borders.

Inevitably, such a shift has caused a lot of disruptions. One of the disruptions is that manufacturing jobs are moving to China and other parts of the world. With unemployment rates in the United States as high as 10 percent in recent years, this is a legitimate concern.

The latest data show that the United States is still the largest manufacturer in the world in terms of output. In 2009, the United States produced 19.9 percent of the world's manufacturing output, compared with 18.6 percent for China.[62] Contrary to the conventional view, manufacturing in the United States has been growing in the past two decades despite the decline in manufacturing jobs. This means that the United States is producing goods with higher value, such as airplanes and medical equipment.

Most American jobs lost to China are low-skilled jobs. By outsourcing those low-skilled jobs to China, Americans have actually become more competitive in high-skilled jobs such as management, innovation, and marketing. The low-skilled jobs also serve the Chinese well, as China's rural migrants are able to move up from no-skill to some-skill jobs.

In recent years, some manufacturing jobs have returned to the United States because of rising wages in China and other developing countries. However, Americans' strength has been and will continue to be in high-skilled jobs and innovation. The United States should focus on creating the new high-value technologies, goods, and businesses needed for our ever-changing world.

Oneness in modernization requires us to see things beyond our immediate interests. Sometimes, our immediate interests are not met, or may even be hurt. Because of the oneness of the world, what benefits others, in reality, also benefits us, although it may be indirect and not readily apparent.

Globalization has benefited China enormously. It is catching up with Western countries and is achieving in just decades what the West took over one hundred years to accomplish. Hundreds of millions of Chinese rural migrant workers earn more and have a higher standard of living, and hundreds of millions more are entering the rank of the middle class.

For developed nations, consumers are able to afford goods at lower prices and enjoy lower inflation. According to Morgan Stanley, American consumers have saved at least $600 billion every year by buying products from China. A study by the Institute for International Economics shows that the United States is as much as $70 billion richer each year because of its relationship with China.[63] For example, when Apple sells a $299 iPod (designed in California and assembled in China), the American computer company makes an $80 profit, while the Chinese assembly plant makes just $4.[64]

If we can adopt the viewpoint of "oneness of the world," it is apparent that the growing global economy increases total economic activity, opportunities, and jobs. As more and more people around the world contribute their labor to producing goods, services, or knowledge of value to others, whether for their neighbor down the street or someone on the other side of the globe, the global economy will expand.

PART II

COMPLEXITIES AND CHALLENGES

CHAPTER 4

A New Economic Engine

"No generation has had the opportunity, as we now have,
to build a global economy that leaves no one behind."

– BILL CLINTON

෬

S an Francisco International Airport is one of my favorite airports in the world. It is nicely carpeted, has exquisite art displays, and features an impressive range of luxury goods in duty-free shops. The best thing about flying internationally, for me, is to indulge myself at the airport duty-free stores. Almost invariably, I would pick up some perfume or Swarovski jewelry.

On one of my trips to China, after passing through the security check, I went into the first duty-free store I saw on the concourse—Gucci. A pair of sunglasses immediately tempted me. It was chic, stylish, and looked perfect on me. It was not too expensive either: $150. There was only one problem: I had just bought a pair of sunglasses by Juicy Couture which I absolutely adored. I certainly did not need two pairs of fancy sunglasses, did I?

As I was debating whether I should get the Gucci sunglasses, I overheard some women speaking my native tongue, Mandarin. I turned around and saw two middle-aged Chinese women who were trying on different pairs of shoes. They did not strike me as upper class or fashionable. However, I noticed the Louis Vuitton handbags they both carried. A teenage boy, looking bored while waiting for the women to shop, sat on a bench with his legs stretched out to show off a pair of Gucci gym shoes. They were the coolest gym shoes that I had ever seen—with red and green stripes and a unique pattern that is only Gucci's. I could only imagine how expensive they were (if they were not knock-offs)!

As I started to get interested, I heard one of the women ask her friend, "Do they look good on me?" She tilted her head, admiring the leather shoes on her slightly swollen feet.

"Very pretty, very pretty," her friend nodded with approval.

"How much do they cost?" the woman asked the sales lady. Unmistakably, almost all the salesladies in the luxury duty-free stores at the airport were Asians and spoke Mandarin.

"Four hundred seventy-five dollars," the saleslady said, looking at the price tag.

The woman turned to her friend and asked, "Shall I get them?"

"Get them, get them," the friend encouraged her.

That was it. She purchased the $475 shoes without the slightest sign of hesitation as if she was just ordering an ice cream. I must confess that I am fond of shoes and have more shoes than I need. Living in a consumer culture in the United States, I find it hard to resist the many temptations. However, I have never owned a pair of shoes that costs remotely close to that price.

After the women and boy left, I chatted with the saleslady and learned her family was originally from Taiwan.

"The Chinese have money now," she said. "Yesterday, I sold a $1,200 purse to a woman from China. She bought the purse for her daughter, who is studying in college here. She wanted her daughter to impress their neighbors when they return home— look who just came back from the United States."

"Isn't that insane?" I said. "Most people in America cannot afford a purse for $1,200."

"Well, it's just like people from Taiwan thirty years ago." She did not seem so surprised. "When people in Taiwan became rich, they were like that, too, buying some expensive luxury goods to show off."

According to Merrill Lynch & Co., China had more than three hundred thousand millionaires, who controlled some $350 billion in assets.[65] Average urban income increased more than 21 percent in recent years. However, exact income is hard to gauge. Many state companies give big bonuses that often they do not report. Some even have benefits that include company-paid overseas travel (solely for tourism). A recent study by Credit Suisse AG revealed that China's households hide as much as $1.4 trillion of income that is not reported in official figures.[66]

As I was about to leave the store, the saleslady smiled charmingly. "By the way, are you still interested in the sunglasses? They look so good on you."

Suddenly, the $150 sunglasses felt quite affordable. So I said, "Okay, I'll get them."

I boarded the plane and settled into my seat in the exit row in economy class. As a premier member of United Airlines, I always try to get a seat in the exit row that provides more leg room. As I plugged my earphones into my iPod and flipped through some magazines, the woman who bought the Gucci shoes walked down the aisle, carrying many plastic bags of duty-free goods. The teenage boy followed her.

Before they settled into the row behind me, the woman pulled out at least a dozen fancy boxes of Gucci, Fendi, and Versace products from the bags and tried to stuff them into her luggage. If I could afford a pair of $475 shoes, I thought, I would be sitting in first class. Naturally, I started a casual conversation. It turned out that she worked in the government judiciary in Beijing. She and her son, who was busy playing computer games in his seat, were with a tourist group that had toured eight U.S. cities in twelve days.

"Well, you must have done pretty well in China," I said. "Look at all these duty-free goodies!"

"They are for my friends," she said. "They gave me a shopping list before I came."

"I see," I said, putting on a smile and trying to sound friendly. "Most Americans cannot afford the shoes you bought at the Gucci store."

"Oh," she said, looking at me cautiously. "Our salaries have been increased three times in the past year."

This story may be an extreme case. However, as incomes in urban China have increased multifold, many people can afford goods and services previously unavailable to them.

While Americans have consumed their way into a deep hole, the Chinese have just begun to open their wallets. News headlines have focused on China's generally weak consumption. The trend in consumption, however, is significantly moving upward. Retail spending has increased steadily at 15 percent and more in recent years. Even during the worldwide recession in 2008-2009, Chinese consumer confidence remained high despite thousands of factories shutting down due to slow global demand. China has already become the world's largest market for automobiles, television sets, and cell phones, and the world's second largest market for luxury goods.

This trend will likely continue. Over the next two decades, the Chinese middle class will begin to play a larger role in China's economy. Studies indicate that the Chinese middle class will wield enormous spending power as it reaches 600 million to 800 million people in less than ten years.[67] As their incomes rise, so will consumption. A 2011 Credit Suisse report predicts China's consumer market will reach $16 trillion by 2020, overtaking the United States as the world's largest consumer market in the world.

As this process unfolds, the Chinese middle class will change the dynamics of the world we live in. The world will not be "China produces and the United States consumes." The Chinese middle class will create enormous opportunities for Western companies to sell into China. This process will serve to better balance global trade.

China's New Consumers

Zhou Jie, the executive manager of a state-owned news media company, enjoyed a typical upper-middle-class lifestyle. As a state employee, Zhou earned a decent salary of about $1,500 a month. Although low by Western standards, in China it is a good income. In addition, his wife, Grace, had a small advertising firm, which helped the family build up some assets. The state-private career arrangements of husband and wife worked out well in China's situation. They were able to tap into opportunities in the thriving private sector without losing significant benefits from the state, such as health insurance and pensions.

Zhou Jie, his wife, and their two daughters lived in a spacious townhouse in Beijing that they had bought a few years before. They shopped for groceries at a local Carrefour, a French supermarket chain, and ate at Pizza Hut, which Chinese consider upscale, with its trendy décor like that of fusion-food restaurants found in California. On weekends, they drove their Volkswagen SUV to the outskirts of Beijing for picnics. During holiday seasons, they vacationed at Hainan Island, the Chinese equivalent of Hawaii, traveled to different parts of the country for sightseeing, or sometimes went overseas.

Like some new middle-class families, Zhou Jie and Grace had their second child despite the government's one-child policy. The penalty for having a second child could be as high as 100,000 yuan ($14,000), depending on the couple's income. However, Zhou Jie and his wife managed to have the fee waived by using their good connections with the government. Chinese call this "going through the back door." I know some of my friends have had to do the same thing in order to have their second child. In the West, we consider it bribery. In China, it has become the way society functions.

Although Zhou Jie felt a lot of pressure raising two children while paying a mortgage, he was quite amazed by how his life had changed. "In 1992, I went to the University of Hawaii as a visiting scholar," he said. "I remember seeing cars racing through the streets and along the highways, and I felt dizzy. It was such a different world. I could not imagine that someday I myself would drive a car."[68]

While Zhou Jie was in Hawaii, his then-girlfriend Grace started an advertising business in Beijing. "One day, I received a phone call from her," Zhou said. "She told me that she and her partner rented a hotel room for 60,000 yuan ($8,600) as an office for their business. I was making only $20 a month. Sixty thousand yuan was an astronomical number to me. I could not comprehend what one could do with that much money."

Now, not only was Zhou Jie driving, but he and his wife owned two cars, a new townhouse, and an old apartment, which they rented to a relative. They enrolled their seven-year-old daughter, Emma, in an international school. The tuition alone cost $20,000 a year. After their second child was born, Grace spent more time taking care of the children while supervising her business from home. "The second child doesn't have Beijing *hukou*," Zhou sighed. "So she cannot get into public school. Private schools are very expensive, and most middle-class people cannot afford private schools." *Hukou* is the household registration system that allows urban residents to have state-subsidized public education and other social welfare benefits.

The couple were determined to send their children overseas for college when they grew up. In the meantime, Zhou Jie was looking for opportunities in the private sector in order to bring in more income. "All of this happened in the last fifteen years," Zhou Jie said. "It's just amazing!"

Many middle class Chinese are influenced by the American way of life and attracted to Western lifestyles. They are bombarded by many material temptations and proliferating choices. TV commercials, the Internet, and Hollywood movies give them a rosy picture of the American middle class. One Chinese blog described it this way: "American middle class people live in a villa with a two-car garage in the suburbs. In front of the house, there is a green lawn. They have 2-3 children, and a dog. The husband goes out to work, and the wife stays at home taking care of the children. They work hard to send their children to college. On weekends, they drive their SUVs to the countryside for barbecues and camping." That is the picture in most Chinese people's minds of "the American Dream"— owning a big house, driving a nice car, and having a comfortable life. The Chinese middle class wants it all.

Walking on the streets of China's bustling cities, one can easily witness prosperity and the consumer boom. Xujia District in west Shanghai, erected from the ruins of abandoned state-owned factories, has become a shopping mecca. Tall department store buildings inundated with thousands of boutique stores and mom-and-pop shops sell familiar global brands like Nike and DKNY. Here you can find everything from jewelry to digital cameras and automobiles within a five-minute walk. Its famous "digital plaza" shelves contain a variety of electronic products, from mobile phones to game consoles. Stores without Western pedigrees sell Burberry bags and Dunhill shirts. Young couples dressed to the nines contemplate the latest computers and BMWs. On average, about eight hundred thousand people visit the shops daily.[69]

Chinese consumer spending has been increasing steadily in recent years. Automobile sales in China have soared from two million in 2003 to over 19 million in 2011.[70] More than four hundred large malls have been built in China since 2000. China is on track to have seven of the world's ten largest shopping malls.[71]

Zhu Yiping, a young entrepreneur who started Herbella, a Chinese version of Victoria's Secret, told me that young Chinese consumers are quick to accept new brands and new products because they have no consumer habits inherited from their parent's generation. For example, men's dress-shirt maker Perfect Products Group (PPG) enjoyed a huge success when it launched a marketing campaign that used top-name celebrities to brand medium-priced products targeting white-collar workers. "That's where the potential is," Zhu said. "Although most of them didn't care about brand, more and more are starting to have brand awareness."[72]

One force driving the consumption boom is that the Chinese are very status conscious. As their financial situation improves, they like to purchase items that increase their status. They are also under considerable peer pressure and feel the need to buy products their friends and neighbors have so as "not to be left behind." They want to own homes, buy cars, and travel for vacations. However, for products and services that their friends and neighbors cannot see, they can be very price-conscious. For example, the woman who bought $475 Gucci shoes would not spend more money on first class airfare.

The younger generation, who cannot afford houses or cars, would buy Louis Vuitton purses or fashionable mobile phones to showcase their status. Many of them live with their parents before they get married (some even after they marry) and usually do not have housing and other daily expenses. They can afford to spend all their incomes on luxury goods that make them feel good.

To show how powerful this kind of peer pressure can be, on a recent trip to China I dug out my Omega watch that I almost never wear in the States, polished it, and put it on my wrist. I have always thought that I am more individualistic than many of my Chinese peers. In the United States, I usually shop at boutique stores and try to dress in a unique style that is only me. However, whenever I go to China, I feel I have to "keep up with the Joneses." Each time I pack my suitcase for China, I scrutinize my wardrobe and frown at some of my not-so-trendy outfits. In the end, my fragile sense of individuality gave in. In order to keep up with increasingly fashionable Chinese women, I packed a Versace shirt that I bought in Cancun and a pair of dressy Italian pants purchased on the Magnificent Mile in Chicago. They looked so out of place among my favorite jeans.

Chinese consumers' spending patterns are expanding to service industries, as Chinese splurge on travel and entertainment. In a 2007 survey, middle-class Chinese said they belonged to fitness clubs, dined out three times a week, and traveled within China twice a year for pleasure.[73] Because China was closed for half a century, many Chinese also desire to see the outside world. They make traveling abroad one of their primary goals in life. In 1993, when I took a trip to Italy, people mistook me for Japanese, as there were many Japanese tourists in Europe in those days but few Chinese. In 2007, I went to Egypt and met many Chinese tourists. Most of them were in their twenties and early thirties, touring the pyramids and posing for photographs with their fingers showing a "victory" sign.

In recent years, some have taken up expensive sports, such as skiing. In the winter of 2008-2009, about three million middle class Chinese went skiing, a sport that was unavailable only fifteen years before. China now has around three hundred ski runs, including some in the subtropical south where people can ski indoors. At Nanshan Ski Village, a ski resort near the northern city of Harbin, they manufacture snow from wells deep underground. Every weekend, IT executives, bankers, and media literati pack the resort.[74]

Changes in consumption habits are evident in the exploding use of consumer credit cards. In 2005, there were thirteen million credit cards in China. Only five years later, the number had increased to more than 200 million. Experts believe that China will likely have 800 million to 900 million credit cards in issue by 2020. Online shopping is increasing dramatically, aided by the increased use of credit cards. One hundred and forty-five million of China's half billion Internet users shopped online in 2011.[75]

The real growth potential lies in China's smaller cities and towns. Since 2006, GDP growth in second- and third-tier cities has exceeded growth in the first-tier cities. It is estimated that about 400 million new Chinese consumers will come from third- and fourth-tier cities like Hefei and Zhengzhou. These consumers will follow the model of the middle class in first- and second-tier cities, demanding products and services that were previously unavailable to them.

On a trip to Chengdu, a second-tier city in south-western China with a population of 5 million, I was struck by the ostentatious signs of Louis Vuitton and Cartier in its downtown. According to Chengdu Retail Industry Association, Chengdu is home to 80 percent of international luxury brands and ranked third behind Beijing and Shanghai in luxury sales.

A cover story in *Chengdu Today*, "Global Luxury Brands Stride Forward in Chengdu," revealed that Chengdu municipal government had set a goal to bring "twenty famous international brands to Chengdu every year" and "by 2015, more than 80 percent of international first-tier brands will have reached western China."

In 2010, Chengdu's retails sales reached $5.8 billion. Much of it went to luxury brands such as Hermes, Burberry and Prada. Louis Vuitton alone registered record sales of $138 million. Cartier generated more revenue in Chengdu than in any other city in China.

When I left China 20 years ago, I was considered too "bourgeois" because I liked to put on pretty clothes while others still wore Mao suits. Those days are long gone. Today, not being "bourgeois" is a subject of public ridicule. As the cover story describes, Chinese consumers consider buying luxury goods a symbol of "paying attention to details and pursuing quality of life."

I had an interesting conversation with the magazine's editor Eureka Wang. Knowing that I had written a book about the Chinese middle class, she asked me if middle class Americans are also fanatically buying luxury goods. I said "very rare." She was surprised. "Who is buying luxury goods in America then?" she asked. "The very rich," I said. This is the difference in luxury consumption between China and the United States.

McKinsey & Co., the global strategic consulting firm, indicates that China will overtake Japan to become the world's largest luxury goods market by 2015. I would expect China could take the crown sooner than that. With a supportive government and status conscious crowds pressured to chase their luxury dreams, global luxury brands can be certain to enjoy phenomenal success in China.

Major Obstacles to Increasing Consumption

A major hindrance to increased Chinese consumption is the country's famously high household saving rate of about 25 percent.[76] Most people I talked to save 25 to 50 percent of their monthly income for a rainy day. One reason for the high saving rate is lack of a social safety net. The government no longer provides cradle-to-grave benefits as it did under the old system. In essence, people set aside large chunks of their income to self-insure against health care costs, as well as save for retirement and their children's educations.

Another factor in the high saving rate is that the consumer finance sector is underdeveloped in China. Chinese banks are less sophisticated than their Western counterparts are and provide limited loan offerings.[77] Traditionally, Chinese consumers tend to avoid spending on borrowed money. Most transactions are cash based; even some large-ticket purchases like cars are commonly paid for with cash. However, informal banking is active. Instead of getting loans from a bank, people often borrow money from their family, friends, and relatives.

The third factor in the high saving rate is a culture of frugality, which is inherited from a history of poverty and a scarcity of resources. Older middle class Chinese still regard "luxury" as a synonym for "unnecessary waste." They are much more conservative than the younger generation and prefer to cut back on spending rather than become indebted.

Major challenges remain before the Chinese middle class can consume more. As Zhou Jie told me, "It will take another twenty years before China can have a stable social safety net to ensure a large and stable middle class." The Chinese government understands the challenges and is taking steps to establish a stronger social safety net. The government's ambitious health care reform to ensure basic health care coverage for 90 percent of the Chinese population is a first step in the right direction. China also announced a plan to subsidize consumption of durable goods by rural households, which could help close the increasing income gap between urban and rural dwellers. Stephen Roach, Morgan Stanley Asia's chairman, believed that if the Chinese government moved aggressively on developing social security, pensions, and nationwide medical care, consumption could achieve a 50 percent share of GDP within five years. [78]

Younger Generation Are Spenders

Younger generations are embracing new economic ideas and lifestyles. Salaries for young Chinese ages twenty to thirty almost tripled in less than a decade. They are "shopaholics" and save next to nothing. Especially, those born after 1980 are lavish spenders who are dramatically different from their parents. They are quite willing to acquire debt to support their spending.

The best person to talk to about young Chinese consumers is probably Shaun Rein, the managing director of China Market Research Group (CMR). His firm has conducted numerous surveys and studies on Chinese consumption habits, especially of young consumers. Rein and I had exchanged e-mails because of our common interest in the Chinese middle class. While in Shanghai, I phoned Rein, and the next thing I knew we were meeting at Starbucks in Xintiandi in central Shanghai.

Xintiandi, or New Heaven and Earth, was constructed out of restored traditional brick stone houses of old Shanghai and adorned with modern cafes, upscale restaurants, boutique shops, and art galleries. It is a place where one can feel nostalgic about the past and simultaneously envision the future. A favorite location for both expats and modish young Chinese, Xintiandi is also an example of the fusion of Eastern and Western culture in Shanghai.

Shaun Rein was at the forefront of studying the emerging Chinese consumers. He recommended that I visit Plaza 66, a luxury mall in Shanghai which features top European brands. When I went there, I was surprised to see that most customers in the mall were young people in their early twenties. "It is the secretaries who make 3,000 yuan a month ($440) who buy these luxury goods," Rein said. "They are buying for status."

A 2008 survey of young adults, ages eighteen to thirty-two, in six cities in China found that 70 percent had spent all their income and had saved nothing in the past year.[79] Most credit card holders in China were under thirty-three.[80]

Rachel Sun is a beautiful young woman who has the most daring dreams. Born in 1983 in Liaoning province, Rachel is one of those "one-child" children in China who are known for their sweet narcissism and wild optimism. At the age of seventeen, she went to Shenzhen, the booming city erected from a fishing village just north of Hong Kong. After junior college, she worked in a company that makes smart-card machines. Smart cards are widely used in China as a combination of credit and debit card with a special security chip embedded in the card for business transactions. As a customer service representative, Rachael earned a salary of 4,800 yuan ($700) per month. However, she owned a tiny apartment, for which she spent half of her salary to pay the mortgage.

"My mother was shocked when she learned that I bought an apartment," she said. "I borrowed some money from my friend and got a loan from the bank. I didn't think it was a big deal."

After work, Rachel likes to go for a massage, drink beer, and dine out with friends at good restaurants. She showed me her pink

Nokia cell phone that hung around her neck like a necklace. "I like mobile phones and computers," she said. "This is my eleventh mobile phone. I change my phone every six months."

"That is really a cute phone," I said. "What would you like to do in the future?"

"I am young and I want to try out different things before I am thirty." Her eyes sparked with passion like those of the young Elizabeth Taylor. "I want to work in Hong Kong or Shanghai to make more money. You know, for money, I am always hungry. I want to go to Paris for Christmas, and I want to go to Bali to play golf."

Today, young Chinese couples preparing to get married are looking for trendy appliances such as large-screen LCD TVs, washing machines with steam wash, and robot vacuum cleaners. Many of them prefer Western brands because of their quality and reputation. Zhao Hong, a marketing manager in Shenzhen, drives a Buick, chats on an iPhone, eats at McDonald's, and wears Nikes.

I visited IKEA in Shanghai. Young couples shopping for furniture and household appliances for their new homes packed the 360,000-square-foot store. It is the second-largest IKEA store in Asia after the one in Malaysia, with almost one thousand parking spaces. On its opening day, it attracted nearly eighty thousand people. The store offers more than seven thousand products and features a five-hundred-seat restaurant and a spacious and colorful children's playground. Its showroom displays, which are absent in traditional Chinese department stores, give people many ideas for how to furnish a beautiful home. The products' modern styles, functionality, and reasonable prices attract Chinese consumers. In 2007, IKEA saw a 38 percent increase in China sales and planned to open more stores in China's second-tier cities, such as Nanjing, Wuhan, and Dalian.[81]

Before I left Shanghai, I thought that I might as well do some shopping for myself. As I roamed the streets of Shanghai, the variety of consumer goods truly overwhelmed me. Nanjing Road and Huihai Avenue, two major streets with department stores and shops, were so crowded that people often bumped into each other. As evening approached, I took off my Gucci sunglasses and carefully put them into my Calvin Klein handbag and zipped it. As I was window-shopping along the street, I felt my handbag move slightly. I immediately became alert because someone had robbed me before. I grabbed my handbag, but found the zipper was open. I panicked—all my work, my notebook and recorder with many days' interviews and notes, my wallet with all my credit cards, not to mention my iPod and sunglasses, were all in the bag. I searched the handbag with horror, not knowing what to think. I guess I must have reacted quickly before the pickpocket could go further. The only thing missing was my new Gucci sunglasses. Everything else was still safely in the bag.

Later that day, I instant-messaged my husband in the United States, telling him how upset I was to have lost my brand new sunglasses.

"You were lucky," he messaged back. "If anything else was stolen, it would have been much worse. Can you imagine if you had lost your notebook or recorder, or your wallet?"

I felt better. I did not need the sunglasses anyway.

In a follow-up e-mail to Shaun Rein, I expressed my concern about the extravagant spending of young Chinese consumers, and wondered if they would follow the footsteps of their American counterparts to consume beyond their means. Rein seemed unconcerned. "We found young couples have a healthy saving rate at about 15 percent," he wrote. He believed that the overall saving rate would fall from 25 to 20 percent by 2030,[82] which is consistent with my research. McKinsey & Co. predicts the household saving rate will fall lower faster, to 15 percent by 2025.

An Alternative Growth Engine

As China rebalances its economy toward domestic consumption, the Chinese middle class will become a powerful alternative growth engine for Western companies as well as the world economy. China is already contributing more to global GDP growth than the United States. [83] In the first half of 2010, when the United States and other Western economies were struggling to recover from the economic downturn, China's economy grew blisteringly at more than 10 percent, surpassing Japan as the world's second largest economy[84].

China's increased domestic consumption will likely boost its imports dramatically in the coming years. Between 2005 and 2008, China's imports from the United States increased almost 70 percent, while exports to the United States grew 38 percent for the same period. Now China is the United States' third largest export market after Canada and Mexico.[85] *The Economist* predicts that China will become the world's largest importer by 2014.

Multinationals, ranging from retailers to automakers, from tourism to banking and financial services, have already made forays into this potentially huge market. Almost every major American company has gone to China, and many of them have already enjoyed huge success.

In 2008, more Buicks were sold in China than in the United States.[86] While General Motors (GM) filed for Chapter 11 bankruptcy in the United States, its sales of all car brands in China had soared. In 2011, GM sold more than 2.5 million vehicles in China, a significant increase from previous years.[87] The government's tax rebate for small-engine and fuel-efficient cars certainly helped sales. GM is now China's top automaker. Its sales in China account for a quarter of its global sales.[88] According to Kevin Wale, GM China Group president, the majority of first-time car buyers come from China's second- and third-tier cities.

GM China has also done a better job of truly listening to customers than GM North America has. For example, it is common for middle class Chinese to have chauffeurs because labor rates are still very affordable. GM's Cadillac SLS model, introduced at a Beijing auto show, addresses the needs of the Chinese market for a roomy, luxurious back seat for chauffeur-driven riders. Other foreign automakers like Volkswagen and Ford are already enjoying huge success in China. Analysts believe demand in China will stay strong for the foreseeable future.

Walmart is another example of how Western companies have benefited from the burgeoning Chinese middle class. Ed Chan, Walmart China CEO, has cited China as a once-in-a-lifetime opportunity for companies that want to sell to its market and the best place on earth to export U. S. products. Walmart opened its first China stores in the southern Chinese city of Shenzhen in 1996, and the Arkansas-based American retail giant is now employing more than ninety thousand associates in 260 outlets throughout China, ranging from its classic Supercenters to retail partnerships with local Chinese retailer Trust-Mart. For Walmart, China represents the biggest opportunity since it saturated America. Retail analyst Bill Dreher of Deutsche Bank Securities also believes that China will be "as big and as successful a market for Walmart as the United States." [89]

Other Western retailers such as Carrefour are rolling out nationwide store networks. The newcomer Auchan, a privately owned French retailer of food and consumer products, is opening, on average, two new stores per month.[90] British home-improvement chain B&Q, which established its first store in China in only 1999, planned to have seventy-five outlets across the country. French women's fashion retailer Trois Suisses (3S) has successfully sold its stylish and affordable clothes via mail order and online sales to large and small cities in China. Other multinationals that have enjoyed huge success in China include Swiss luxury watchmaker Omega, German sportswear brand Adidas, and French cosmetics company L'Oreal.

In the food industry, the phenomenal success of Kentucky Fried Chicken is another example for Western companies that want to reap the enormous benefits of the Chinese middle class. In a country that has thousands of years of distinctive culinary history and millions of local restaurants, Kentucky Fried Chicken, known as KFC, has become the single largest restaurant chain in China, with nearly 2,600 restaurants in over 550 cities. One of the secrets of its success is that Kentucky Fried Chicken positioned itself in China as a Western brand with Chinese characteristics. It has highly localized menus, including congee, or Chinese-style porridge, for breakfast, Peking duck served with scallion and seafood sauce, and *you tiao,* or Chinese dough fritters. It is embraced by young and old alike and appeals to both Chinese family-style dining and fun get-togethers with friends. Besides KFC, other restaurant chains under Louisville, Kentucky-based conglomerate Yum! Brands, such as Pizza Hut and Taco Bell restaurants, all have better-than-expected earnings and are opening one to two restaurants a day in China.[91]

There are many other examples of foreign companies enjoying huge success in the China market. Nike has become China's number one sports brand. In 2009, Nike's revenue in China increased 22 percent, compared with only 2 percent in the United States. The NBA's thirty thousand Chinese retails stores were selling 60 percent more merchandise in 2009 than the previous year. The revenue of Caterpillar, a California-based construction and mining equipment maker, grew from $700,000 in 2005 to $2.6 billion in 2009. Logistics companies such as DHL have registered annual growth rates of 35 percent-45 percent in recent years as China's highways tripled in less than ten years from about 12,000 miles in 2000 to more than 37,000 miles in 2009.

Service sector firms, previously hindered by government restrictions, are also beginning to make their mark. In the last few years, foreign asset management firms have begun to sell investment funds in China, and international accounting firms have been seeking to strengthen their presence in Chinese cities. International banks like HSBC and Citigroup, although still heavily restricted, have established retail networks. U.S. insurance firm Liberty Mutual started its China general-insurance venture in Chongqing, a huge municipality in the west of the country.[92]

As Michael Bloomberg wrote in "A Race We Can All Win," "I believe that China is not a threat to America, but an opportunity. An incredible opportunity...Just as a growing American economy is good for China, a growing Chinese economy is good for America. That means we have a stake in working together to solve common problems, rather than trying to browbeat or intimidate the other into action. And it means we should seize on opportunities to learn from one another."[93]

A virtuous circle is being established. As incomes continue to rise, as more middle class Chinese feel they can afford more discretionary spending, more money will flow to consumption. In turn, this will stimulate further growth and employment in the economy, and even further consumption. China's growth into a major consumer economy will be good for people in other countries because China's consumer markets will generate enormous opportunities for companies around the world, creating jobs, expanding trade, and leading to a more balanced global economy. The world will be able to thrive on the virtuous circle of globalization without being as vulnerable to an American recession.

Myth of China as a Superpower

Even with such dramatic growth, it will take some time for the Chinese middle class to become a majority of China's population. It is important to point out that the Chinese middle class, although estimated at three hundred million strong in 2011, is only 25 percent of China's entire population. The average income of the Chinese middle class is, and will continue to be, lower than the average income of the middle class in Western countries in dollar terms. Even if the Chinese middle class grows to be as massive as predicted—say, 700 million by 2020—it will still only constitute about 50 percent of China's total population because of population growth. China will not become a consumer economy like the United States. However, the Chinese economy will be more balanced, as the middle class is providing the impetus to move the economy towards more consumption and less reliance on investment and exports.

The rise of a large Chinese middle class is coming at a time when the middle class in the West is increasingly insecure. Many people in the West believe that China is already a superpower, or will quickly replace the United States to become a superpower. A recent poll by the Pew Research Center reveals that 44 percent of Americans believe that China is the world's leading economic power, while, in reality, China's economy is only one-half the size of the U.S. economy.[94] This kind of misconception has engendered many unrealistic fears about China.

I believe that the concept of superpower is outdated. It is based on America's mentality of dominance. In today's increasingly flattened world, no single country can dominate. Moreover, dominance is not true leadership. Nevertheless, for the sake of discussion, I would like to quote the definition of superpower by Fareed Zakaria, renowned journalist and CNN host. Zakaria defined in his best-selling book *The Post-American World* that a superpower is a country that achieves dominance in ideas or ideology, an economic system, and military power.

In terms of ideas or ideology, the Chinese are probably more confused than anyone else in the world. The Cultural Revolution destroyed many Chinese traditions, including Confucianism. Communism has proved to be disastrous, and no one believes in it anymore. In today's China, where money is king, people have become disillusioned with any notion of ideals. There has been serious moral decay in society.

In recent years, the Chinese government has called for building "a harmonious society." Harmony is a virtuous concept deeply rooted in Chinese culture and the Confucian tradition. It could become a new ideology for China. However, propaganda has overused it, turning it into a cliché rather than a meaningful ideal.

The United States remains the country standing for the universal ideals that people around the world aspire to—liberty and democracy. Unlike Americans who have a clear message for the world, the Chinese do not have a vision for themselves, let alone to influence the world. I have talked to Chinese officials, scholars, businesspeople, and students. None of them sees China as a super-power. In contrast, many of them look up to the United States as a model and admire the American way of life.

Economically, China's achievements are indeed impressive. In the past thirty years, China has sustained nearly double-digit growth. However, we need to keep in mind that China started from a very low level of GDP. Much of its growth comes from heavy investment in infrastructure. In 2011, China's per capita GDP was about $8,000, compared with $46,000 in the United States.[95] Among the world's ten largest companies, the United States claims five, and China has none.[96]

With all the troubles on Wall Street, it is easy to forget that China's economic success is actually a triumph of capitalism. In recent decades, China has been learning from the West and now primarily practices capitalism. Although China is searching for a recipe that suits the country's unique situation, namely a "social-ist market economy with Chinese characteristics," it has been a trial-and-error exercise. China has not yet established an economic model that has proven it can withstand long-term tests.

In 2010, China surpassed Japan to become the world's second largest economy. Some people believe that China will eventually surpass the United States as the world's largest economy. Others argue that the line between the United States and China may never be crossed. I believe that China's economy will slow down when its per capita income approaches $10,000. That will make China's economy close to the size of the U. S. economy.

Militarily, China's military spending is only a fraction of what the United States spends. A 2009 Pentagon report estimated China's total military spending at between $105 billion and $150 billion, compared to $719 billion by the United States. Until recently, China did not have a foreign policy or a global strategy.

Even its current foreign policies are focused almost exclusively on commerce.

Harvard professor Joseph Nye, former dean of the Kennedy School, has an in-depth analysis about whether China will become a contender with the United States.[97] He believes that China is not likely to become a peer competitor to the United States on a global basis. However, he warns that China could challenge the United States in Asia, "and the dangers of conflict can never be ruled out."

However, I think China's influence in Asia will be limited. Who is China's ally? North Korea? Singapore? India is more likely to be allied with the United States than with China, and we know Japan's position. As much as I love China, I have to agree with Singaporean scholar Simon Tay's comment: "No one in Asia wants to live in a Chinese-dominated world. There is no Chinese dream to which people aspire."

Many vital functions of Chinese society, including its education and health care systems, are far from sophisticated. China is not yet a country of the rule of law. The government still arbitrarily detains dissidents and censors the Internet. Corruption and nepotism are rampant. Chinese culture tends to reward the mediocre rather than the extraordinary. There are many uncertainties in China's future, including the ramifications of environmental degradation, an aging population, political instability, social strife, and ethnic conflicts.

Despite all the problems the United States faces, I still believe that the United States has stronger long-term political and economic fundamentals than China. However, the United States needs to rethink its global strategy and move away from the Cold War mentality. As Harvard University Distinguished Service Professor Joseph Nye pointed out in his book *The Future of Power*, in the 21st century, America must not "lead over" other nations, but "lead with" other nations. That means the United States needs to get back to the fundamentals that made this a great country to begin with, lead by example, and work with countries that are not American allies. By letting go of its obsession with dominance, America can rise as a true global leader with greater influence.

China is and will continue to be a major economic power. China's presence as a major economic power will be good for the world as well as for the United States, as no one wants to live in an American-dominated world, either. China's strength is that it can be assertive without being confrontational. It is crucial that the United States makes China a partner, not an enemy, because the future of the world's prosperity and stability depends on it.

Interdependence of U.S.-China Economies

Historically, China's economy is driven by investment and export. Consumption, on the other hand, is a mere 36 percent of GDP, compared with 71 percent in the United States.[98] In fact, the share of consumption in China's GDP growth has declined in recent years due to a dramatic increase in infrastructure investment. Although exports are important to China, the biggest driver of China's growth is actually investment. In 2009, exports accounted for only about 10 percent of GDP when factoring in the value-added components of the exports, because much of the value of the exported goods is created elsewhere.[99]

Large imbalances exist in China's economy, just as they do in the U.S. economy. Interestingly, imbalances in both countries mirror each other. On a macroeconomic level, China produces more goods than it consumes. Its GDP growth has been dominated by growth in investment. The United States consumes more than it produces. U.S. GDP growth has depended heavily on borrowing-based consumption and on growth in foreign investment, mostly from China. On a microeconomic level, China has a very high household saving rate, accounting for about 25 percent of its GDP. The United States has been overspending for many years, with a personal saving rate near zero in the years before the worldwide recession hit.[100]

Today, Chinese are worried whether it is a good idea to rely heavily on exports as their sole growth engine. Americans are worried whether it is a good idea to rely heavily on money controlled by a foreign government. When America is in recession, the Chinese are the first ones to feel the pain: waves of factories close and millions of workers lose their jobs. When China tries to preserve its own savings by trying to keep the value of the dollar high, Americans are the first ones to benefit, as their lifetime savings and 401(k) accounts retain their value.

It seems the Chinese and Americans are worried about the opposite sides of the same problem. However, the fact that these imbalances have lasted for such a long time, and at times seemed to serve both countries well, is precisely because of the interdependence of the global economy.

These imbalances have caused geopolitical concerns, trade disputes, and protectionism. In the United States, people are concerned that America does not produce enough goods and depends on China's cheap loans to finance Americans' way of life. In China, people are concerned about the exact opposite problem: millions of jobs depend on the export sector, which is subject to fluctuating demand from Western countries.

China's oversaving has proved to be as much of a problem as the United States' overconsuming. Today, China earns, on average, a real return of 1 percent-2 percent or less on its $2 trillion in reserves. If the money were not being put into reserves—in essence, lent to the United States at such low rates of return—it could have been invested more productively in other projects, earning some 10 percent to 15 percent return. Harvard economist Dani Rodrik estimated that sending so much money abroad instead of investing it domestically costs the Chinese more than $40 billion a year. This money could be used to develop the social safety net and boost domestic consumption.

Both China and the United States need to rebalance their economies. For the United States, the global recession has forced some rebalancing as consumers cut back spending and increase saving. For China, the rebalancing has already begun, as the Chinese middle class is creating stronger domestic demand.

Oneness in Economy: We Are All in This Together

The world economy has become increasingly interrelated. In particular, the United States and China are enmeshed together and have become more interdependent than ever. Bilateral trade between the United States and China has increased dramatically, from $7.6 billion in 1985 to almost $500 billion in 2011. [101] The interdependence of the two economies cannot be more evident than the fact that China holds more than $1 trillion in U.S. government debt.

Yet, large imbalances have strained the mutually beneficial aspects of interdependence. One aspect of these imbalances is that China's currency, the yuan, has been undervalued by 15 percent-25 percent against a weighted average of the currencies used by China's trading partners. By 2011, the U.S. trade deficit with China had grown to $295 billion. [102] The trade deficit has become so large that it is a political issue in the United States. This has caused threats of protectionism in the United States, which can, in turn, cause retaliation and protectionism in China.

Something needs to rebalance both economies, and that process has already begun. In the United States, the global recession provided the incentive for people to spend less and save more. In China, the rise of the middle class is shifting the economy more towards consumption.

As discussed throughout this book, China and the United States have a lot to learn from each other, and can work together to benefit the world as a whole. On a personal level, overspending and oversaving have been taken to extremes in these two large economies. For overspenders, revisiting the virtue of frugality can help them get back to economic fundamentals, such as not spending beyond their means and saving for a rainy day. For oversavers, healthy spending provides another vehicle for robust economic growth. In China, it means raising awareness that the middle class can be more involved in forming policies to improve the social safety net and reduce the need for saving.

On an international level, robust international trade and a strong U.S.-China relationship will be crucial for global stability and prosperity. The American and Chinese economies are inextricably intertwined. Rebalancing the global economy requires China and the United States to join forces as partners because they need each other. While the United States should pressure China to liberalize its exchange rate to reflect market forces, we must oppose any form of protectionism, as it is a recipe for disaster. Trade is the only way to keep growing our way out of our imbalances.

As China's and America's economies become more balanced, they will become even more interdependent as America exports more to China. This will produce more prosperity in both countries, yielding a virtuous circle of more growth, more interdependence, and more balance, driven in good measure by the growth of the Chinese middle class.

As Nobel Prize-winning economist Joseph Stiglitz points out, "Too many people think of economics as a zero-sum game, and that China's success is coming at the expense of the rest of the world. Yes, China's rapid growth poses challenges to the West. Competition will force some to work harder, to become more efficient, or to accept lower profits. But economics is really a positive-sum game. An increasingly prosperous China has not only expanded imports from other countries, but is also providing goods that have kept prices lower in the West, despite sharply higher oil prices in recent years."[103]

Global trade can improve everyone's standard of living by reducing everyone's costs. As each country seeks to discover and leverage its own unique abilities, the world economy benefits as more efficient producers lower everyone's costs, allowing everyone to invest his or her resources more wisely.

This process is inherently disruptive as change inevitably arrives at our doorsteps. It certainly has its unsettling aspects. Changes in the global economy are inevitable as knowledge and technologies spread across the world, countries all over the world modernize, and the world economy becomes more interdependent. There will be many disruptions to geographic regions, companies, and individual lives. We can allow ourselves to feel threatened by these changes, or we can embrace them for the positive aspects they will bring. By seeing this process in its larger context, that of a unifying force that will, over time, actually improve the lives of everyone, we realize that we are in the process of creating a oneness in the world economy where each of us has his or her own unique contribution to make.

CHAPTER 5

Environmental Megachallenge

*"There is a sufficiency in the world for man's need
but not for man's greed."*

- MOHANDAS K. GANDHI

৬৩

On one of my trips to China, I traveled to Chongqing, a fast-growing metropolitan center considered one of the most polluted cities in China. Located in southwest China, where the upper reaches of the Yangtze River join the Jialing River, Chongqing is surrounded by a pinnacled mountain range, with a striking landscape of limestone "forests" of sinkholes, ravines, and caverns known as karst. Historically, Chongqing was perceived as a "mountain city" because of its geological environs.

In recent years, Chongqing has gained significant attention from the central government because of its location at the head of the reservoir of the Three Gorges Dam. In 1997, the government made Chongqing one of only four province-level municipalities (the other three are Beijing, Shanghai, and Tianjin). These special metropolitan areas share an unparalleled level of autonomy, reporting directly to the central government rather than to provincial governors. With completion of the Three Gorges Dam, Chongqing is targeted to be the beachhead for development of the western part of the country. The government wants to transform Chongqing into a "Chinese Chicago" as part of its "Go West Campaign" to open up inland development, as Chicago did in the United States of the nineteenth century.

Chongqing: Nexus of Environmental Challenges

I arrived in Chongqing on the afternoon of May 12, 2008, without knowing about the devastating magnitude-8 earthquake that had just happened less than two hundred miles away. "People are leaving Chongqing," the taxi driver told me. "It was a big earthquake. Even people in Beijing and Shanghai felt it." Beijing and Shanghai are more than three thousand miles away. That was impossible, I thought to myself, and foolishly dismissed the taxi driver's comment as a rumor.

"China has too many people," the taxi driver went on. "It's no big deal if several hundreds or thousands of people die." You would think such comments are insanely inhumane, but that was not the first time I had heard remarks like this in China. Human lives are less venerated when people are in survival mode. The taxi driver was probably a migrant worker from a poor village. For him, staying alive had already given him a sense of dignity.

Approaching the city from the airport, I started to feel claustrophobic. On undulating ground along the Yangtze River, I saw the most densely built high-rises and skyscrapers. Unstylish, they were concrete forests, as if to mirror Chongqing's geographic landscape of "stone forests." The city itself sits on hilly terrain that slopes down into a peninsula embraced by the two rivers. From afar, it looked almost like a fortress. For a moment, I fantasized it was the Tower of Cirth Ungol from Tolkien's *Lord of the Rings*. In fact, the comparison is not too exaggerated, as Chongqing, too, has streets stacking above streets and buildings standing atop buildings.

A dark haze covered Chongqing, as in most cities I visited in China. The sky was gray, streets were gray, and buildings were gray. Noisy traffic shuttled nonstop on dusty streets, adding more stress to what is obviously an already stressed environment. I remember that Wang Jianshuo, the blogger featured in chapter 2, told me that he did not know people were supposed to be able to swim in the rivers. I suspect that some children growing up in China might not know the sky is supposed to be blue.

I only realized how serious the earthquake was after I arrived in downtown Chongqing. It was like a ghost town. Although there was no visible damage, I could sense that people were still in a panic. The streets were empty and all the stores were shut with security bars on doors and windows. Looking around, all I could see were high-rise buildings. Imagine yourself in lower Manhattan, or downtown Chicago, standing in the shadows of the skyscrapers, and you can barely see the sky. Downtown Chongqing is like that, except the streets are narrower and the buildings squeeze more densely against one another. I thought to myself that if there were a serious aftershock, I would definitely be buried among mountains of debris.

As soon as I checked into my hotel, I tried to obtain more information about the earthquake. However, the hotel staff seemed more concerned about the prospect of losing business than their guests' safety. "Don't worry," the young woman at the front desk said. "I am sure it's going to be okay." In a moment like this, I definitely missed America. In the United States, at least I would have been given accurate information about what had happened. I did not plan to leave Chongqing, but I took the precaution to move my room from the twenty-third floor to the tenth floor. I figured that if something did happen, it would be easier for me to walk down the staircase from the tenth floor and have a better chance to survive.

That night, I was physically tired as well as mentally stressed, and fell into a deep sleep. In the middle of the night, I felt my bed shaking violently and heard people in the hallway screaming. Still, I must have been too tired—I thought I had a bad dream and fell back to sleep. The next morning at the buffet breakfast, I overheard people talking about how frightened they were at the aftershock during the night and how they ran out into the street. "What, that was an aftershock?" I said in disbelief. "I thought it was my nightmare."

Things gradually returned to normal the next day. I had a pre-arranged lunch appointment with a couple who are Chongqing natives. The husband, Yu Xin, worked at a software company, and the wife was a loan officer in a local bank. They were among millions of the new middle class who were clearly on their way up. They picked me up at my hotel in their car, bringing with them their newborn son and an *Aiyi*, a rural migrant who took care of the baby. We headed to a nearby hotel that has a revolving rooftop restaurant with a great view of Chongqing.

At lunch, I had a 360-degree view of the city. From there, I could clearly tell that the Chinese are on a building spree. As far as my eyes could see, there was nothing but high-rise after high-rise, with still more under construction.

In its quest for economic development, China seems to have blindly followed the path of Western industrialization. Since the 1980s, the Chinese government had sent its officials to Western countries to study how developed nations had advanced their economies. For example, the Shanghai municipal government wanted to learn from the West how to rebuild Shanghai. Its officials visited New York, Paris, and other top cities in the world. Within ten years, Shanghai became a new Paris with the most spectacular skyscrapers.

It is no surprise that what they learned from those countries was sprawling skylines, private car ownership, and energy-consumptive practices. This statement could not be written more strikingly than it is in Chongqing's downtown: a near-replica of the Empire State Building with a distinctive "New York, New York" sign—the symbol of capitalism—stood, ironically, near the Monument of Liberation—a symbol of the communist victory in 1949.

Yet, the sheer scale and dynamics of Chongqing's development make magnificent, modern cities like New York City or Chicago look outdated. Since 1997, the central government invested $2 billion annually in Chongqing to build a web of new highways, bridges, ports, and railways. In a mere decade, Chongqing transformed into a hustling and bustling metropolis rivaling Shanghai. In 2008, the city of Chongqing had about eight million people. By 2025, Chongqing will likely become one of eight megacities with more than twenty-four million inhabitants.[104]

Mega Pollution: China's Greatest Challenges

China's extraordinary growth has come at a cost. It has caused serious damage to the environment and created concern in a resource-limited world. China has the world's most polluted cities. In 2008, China exceeded the United States to become the number one emitter of greenhouse gases.[105] By 2010, China had overtaken the United States as the world's largest energy consumer.[106]

As hundreds of millions of new members of the middle class demand the same level of comfort enjoyed by people in advanced economies, China will increase its demand for energy and resources, putting more stress on the environment. In the past decade, China has built about 7.5 billion square feet of commercial and residential space each year.[107] In the next twenty years, China will build 430 billion square feet of floor space, the equivalent of ten New York Cities, and will have 55 billion square feet of roads and construct 170 mass-transit systems.[108] The International Energy Agency projects that China's greenhouse emissions will exceed the rest of the world's combined increase by 2020.[109]

A major cause of China's pollution is its high dependence on coal, which it has in abundance. In 2006, China already was burning more coal than the United States, Japan and the European Union combined, and coal consumption was increasing at a rate of 14 percent per year.[110] The coal power plants and thousands of coal-burning factories release enormous quantities of sulfur, polluting the air with toxic chemicals and global-warming gases and causing acid rain that poisons lakes and rivers. More than three-fourths of the country's forests have disappeared. Two-thirds of its six hundred cities fail to meet the country's air quality standards. Only 1 percent of China's urban dwellers breathe air considered safe. [111] Water pollution is severe and deteriorating. Ninety percent of urban rivers are polluted, 62 percent of surface water cannot support fish, and 26 percent is unsuited for any purpose.[112] In addition, about one hundred cities in northern China were suffering severe water shortages.

The pollution has severely affected public health. The poor air quality and polluted rivers continue to take a huge toll in premature deaths. Air pollution is a leading cause of lung disease, cancer, and other diseases.[113] Nearly five hundred million people lack access to safe drinking water. Children are killed or sickened by lead poisoning or other types of local pollution. The World Bank and China's State Environmental Protection Administration (SEPA) released a report in July 2007 indicating that every year, pollution accounts for 750,000 premature deaths.[114] Pollution costs China $100 billion a year, or 5.8 percent of its gross domestic product.[115]

The country has made a big sacrifice for the business boom at the cost of the environment. There was little regard for the waste pumped into rivers and air. Chinese manufacturers that dump waste into rivers or pump smoke into the sky make the cheap products that fill stores in the United States and Europe. Often, foreign companies subcontract to these manufacturers—or even own them.

In the West, when we accuse China of being the rising giant of global warming, we conveniently forget that we have shipped most of our dirty industries to China so that we can buy products more cheaply. Furthermore, foreign investment continues to rise as multinational corporations build more factories in China. *China Daily* reported that pollution causes at least fifty thousand disputes and protests throughout China every year. For example, a proposal for a new chemical factory in the fast-growing city of Xiamen caused a protest outside City Hall by about twenty thousand middle class Chinese, organized by anonymous cell phone text messages. One protester said, "They are making poisonous chemicals for foreigners that the foreigners don't dare produce in their own countries. It is better to die now, forcing them out, than to die of a slow suicide."[116]

China's environmental nightmare has become a global nightmare. China is generating such enormous quantities of pollution that the effects are felt far downwind and cause mortal havoc in societies and ecosystems throughout the world. Acid rain caused by China's sulfur-dioxide emissions severely damages forests and watersheds in Korea and Japan and impairs air quality in California. The environmental loss is already incalculable.

The Government's Commitment

The good news is China's leaders have realized the severity of the problem. They know that as China grows more prosperous, and the Chinese populace buys more homes and cars, China must urgently adopt green technologies; otherwise, it will destroy its environment and its people. Green technology will decide whether China continues on its current growth path or chokes itself to death.

Since 2003, the Chinese government has created a multi-pronged approach to seriously address the environmental problem. The plan addresses energy efficiency, energy sources (coal, nuclear, and renewable), eco-friendly buildings, transportation, and an efficient power grid. As part of its energy efficiency strategy, the Chinese government has targeted a reduction in energy intensity— the amount of energy it takes to produce one yuan of GDP—of 20 percent over three years.[117]

In 2007, China invested 1.35 percent of GDP ($49 billion for 2007) over 2008-2010 in environmental protection, focused on water pollution, air pollution, and solid waste. One intended result was to increase the percentage of large cities with at least 292 days of good air quality per year, from 69 percent in 2005 to 75 percent in 2010. The plan shows a commitment to keep increasing the investment along with increases in GDP growth.

The central government has taken steps to reduce coal-burning pollution. Starting in 2005, the government mandated that all new, large coal power plants must use modern "supercritical" coal-burning technology, which is much more efficient.[118] Besides the new large plants, there are many small and older coal power plants. The government now mandates that *all* coal power plants have scrubbers to remove up to 95 percent of the sulfur.[119] The government is also removing from service the dirtier, inefficient coal power plants. During 2007 alone, over five hundred smaller plants were closed, totaling more than 14 gigawatts of electricity capacity,[120] enough capacity to serve two million American homes, and saving fourteen million metric tons of carbon dioxide emissions.[121]

The government is also addressing vehicle energy efficiency and pollution. Since July 2006, all new automobiles must meet fuel-economy standards stricter than the standards in the United States.[122] The government has issued more than thirty vehicle emissions standards, and is supporting development of alternative energy vehicles and clean fuels.[123]

Challenges Remain

In spite of the central government's policies, there are several major challenges. One challenge is that enforcement and implementation of policies are weak at the local level. Local governments have strong incentives to prioritize economic development over the environment. Most of the targets for energy efficiency and air and water quality in the previous plan, covering 2001-2005, were not achieved. For example, instead of falling, sulfur dioxide emissions rose 28 percent over the five-year period. The explanation given was that energy demand increased 55 percent over the period, much more than expected, and the plan to get coal power plants to adopt scrubbers did not really take hold.[124]

This failing comes back to the central government's sometimes-weak control over local governments. Coal mining is an extremely profitable business which helped grow local economies and most likely helped fatten local officials' wallets. Li Chun-sheng, owner of a building insulation business in Beijing, told me that so-called "coal bosses" are the richest people in town in Shanxi province. "Money blew to them like the wind," Li said. "They literally made a profit of several million yuan in a matter of a day."

It is not surprising that the "Green GDP" initiative, introduced by President Hu Jintao to provide an environmental measure of local officials' performance and to change the culture of "economic growth overrides all," failed, because, in some provinces, the pollution-adjusted growth rates were nearly zero, and local officials simply killed it.[125] Jin Ruidong, director of Natural Resources Defense Council's Beijing office, told me, "If the government tightens up control, everything is dead; but if the government loosens control, everything becomes chaotic."

While traveling in China, I noticed there was not much information about environmental protection at the local level. While there was a lot of propaganda on TV about the Olympics, nation building, and the country's history and civilization, there was not much on green opportunities, green technology, or green propaganda. It was a big contrast with what I saw in California. If China is to become a major power in the world, it needs to stop being narcissistic about its past and look into the future instead. The central government may understand the environmental issues well. At the local level, however, there is not much awareness.

Another aspect of the problem is expectations. Since China has been a top-down system ruled by the central government for decades, people believe the environment is the government's job. Robert Shen, a manager in an Internet company in Hangzhou, had seen Al Gore's *An Inconvenient Truth*. Still, he did not seem to care much about global warming. He told me that he believes in "natural selection"—things will work out by themselves and people do not need to worry about it. Many people told me that as long as their standard of living increases and they have money for the basics, they would eventually begin to care about the environment.

Electric Cars: Turning Crisis into Opportunity

While the challenges are daunting, enormous opportunities exist to turn the crisis around. Studies indicate that replacing the majority of the world's vehicles with hybrids and battery-powered cars would help reduce greenhouse gas emissions by 42 percent by 2030.[126]

No one will deny hundreds of millions of Chinese from pursuing their Chinese dream to have a better life and aspiring to the same standard of living as in affluent countries. When I first came to the United States, I dreamed of having a car so that I could drive wherever I wanted. With my hard-earned waitressing money, I bought my first car, a 1982 diesel-powered Chevette, for only $800. Now, it is hard to imagine what an $800 car could do. Nevertheless, I drove it from New Hampshire to New York City, and even managed to speed at almost 90 miles per hour on the highway without being caught by the police. I simply adored my little car.

That car did not last long, but not because it broke down. Someone hit me at an intersection and destroyed my little Chevette. The front window glass smashed onto my face, and some pieces of glass went into my eyes. Fortunately, I was not badly hurt except for some blood on my face. The person who hit me had actually stolen a car and was apparently driving in great haste. By the time the police and ambulance came, he had already disappeared, with his car pushed into a wall over the sidewalk. (Police caught him a few blocks away.) I had been in the United States for only a few months and did not know how to make an insurance claim. Since I only bought an auto insurance policy to cover accidents that were my fault, I thought my insurance policy did not cover accidents caused by another driver.

A few weeks later, someone from the insurance company called me. She asked me a few questions, and said, "I'm going to make you very happy today." The next thing I knew, a check for $3,500 was in my mailbox. Although people told me later that I could have claimed much more than that amount, I was extremely happy with the $3,500. With that money, I bought my second car, a Toyota.

Millions of Chinese also dream of having their own car. However, if only 20 percent of Chinese drove SUVs, the world would have a big problem. Anyone who has visited China recently would complain about traffic and pollution in Beijing, Shanghai, and other major cities. Car ownership has increased dramatically in recent years. In 2009, China had become the world's largest automobile market, with sales of 13.6 million vehicles. Heavy traffic and use of gasoline engines have made automobiles the leading source of air pollution in China's major cities. China does not have the same luxury as Western countries to pollute its way to prosperity and to clean up later, because later will be too late.

In September 2008, amidst the Wall Street meltdown, little-known Chinese company BYD introduced its F3DM model, the world's first mass-produced plug-in hybrid car. [127] Chinese entre-preneur Wang Chuan-fu started BYD in 1995 as a battery man-ufacturer in Shenzhen. The company went public on the Hong Kong stock exchange in 2002. Since then, BYD has grown rap-idly and has become one of the leading small-battery companies in the world. Its batteries are found in cell phones, digital cameras, iPods, and electric toothbrushes.

The company entered the electric car market in 2003 by purchasing a dying state-owned car manufacturer. Wang, a visionary entrepreneur, saw opportunity in electric cars as environmental problems increasingly became an issue in China's development. He believed that he had a chance to succeed in this field by exploiting BYD's expertise in batteries. His first electric car, unveiled in Detroit in December 2008, ran for about sixty miles purely on battery power. Priced at $22,000, it was expensive for most Chinese. However, the Chinese government provided a $7,300 subsidy for buyers, which covered one-third its price.

America's most successful investor, Warren Buffet, was so impressed with the company's management and its prospects for electric vehicles that he purchased 10 percent of BYD for $230 million,[128] a stake whose value grew to over $1 billion in ten months. Buffet believed that BYD could become one of the world's largest automakers by selling electric cars, according to *Fortune* magazine. BYD will likely be the first Chinese company to sell electric cars in the United States. In 2010, BYD started delivering in China a battery-powered, five-passenger crossover vehicle called the E6, with plans to bring it to the United States.

The company employs some 130,000 people. "We are dreaming big," Xin Jin, a business manager at BYD's Cupertino, California, office, told me. "What we are doing at BYD is not just electric cars. We are also working on battery charging stations and smart grids. In our Shenzhen headquarters compound, we have a green village, called 'Village of the Future,' where we use solar and wind power and recycle rainwater. We are building a green future."[129] When asked what BYD stands for, Xin Jin said, "It stands for 'Build Your Dream.'"

My later research revealed that "BYD" is the initials of the Chinese characters *Bi Ya Di*, which does not mean anything but sounds foreign or Western. Many Chinese companies use Western-sounding names to make their companies or product brands sound modern, or to imply their businesses have Western connections. When Bi Ya Di listed on the Hong Kong Exchange, Wang Chuan-fu wanted to give the company name a visionary touch. He invented the term "Build Your Dream" for BYD to inspire his employees. Some investors joked that BYD might as well stand for "Build Your Dollar." I suppose both make sense.

The Chinese government is aggressive in promoting electric and hybrid cars. Buyers of electric and hybrid cars receive a 3,000 yuan ($440) subsidy.[130] In June 2010, China began paying subsidies of up to 60,000 yuan ($8,784) per car to manufacturers of electric and hybrid vehicles on a trial basis in five cities. The government invested $1.5 billion in research and development on electric and hybrid cars over the period 2009-2011.[131] China's car companies are making good progress. Nanjing IVECO and Chery are both bringing out electric cars.

There are many opportunities for Western companies as well as for cooperation between the United States and China in the electric car market. Transportation accounts for 29 percent of total energy use in the United States. Electric vehicles are an area that could make a difference. McKinsey & Co., a global management consulting firm, predicts that if the United States and China can achieve a penetration of 45 percent electric cars by 2030, electric cars could generate 46 percent of new auto sales, reduce oil imports by 18 percent, and reduce CO_2 emissions by 0.7 gigatons (more than 10% of the United States' total CO_2 emissions).[132] However, this cannot be done unless the United States and China work together to make it happen. Achieving an electric vehicle adoption rate of 45 percent would require significant investment and technology development, mass production capacity, and putting associated infrastructure in place. Only the largest economies have the scale required to accomplish this.

Green Buildings: Turning Crisis into Opportunity

Residential energy demand is rising rapidly as the growing Chinese middle class increasingly can afford homes with modern appliances such as refrigerators and air-conditioners. Since 2000, China's buildings have been growing by nearly 20 billion square feet every year.[133]

Li Yue, a young woman who works at a civil engineering design firm in Chongqing, took me to the condominium she had bought three years earlier. As we drove across the Jialing River to the northern part of the city, Li Yue pointed out new urban residential neighborhoods. "Here were crop fields ten years ago," Li said. Now, hundreds and hundreds of high-rise apartments sprouted up in the area. Each community had a swimming pool, tennis court, and convenience store.

At age twenty-eight, Li earned about 8,000 yuan ($1,250) a month as a civil engineer. Her two-bedroom condominium had an air-conditioner, refrigerator, microwave, washing machine, television, and computer.[134] Most young people her age in America cannot afford to own a home. Yet Li and her fiancé, who was still in his doctoral program, planned to buy another home in the coming year when they were to be married.

"China has the world's toughest problems," Rob Watson, the founding father of LEED, a green building benchmark program, told me. For the past decade, Rob has worked with the Chinese government and was instrumental in developing China's green building standards. "The middle class consumes ten times more than peasants. Even if 20 percent of the Chinese people become middle class, it means adding another United States. It could cause potential disasters." As a scientist, Rob believes that humans should abide by the laws of nature. "If not, there will be serious ramifications and humanity may face catastrophe."[135]

With 350 million people moving from rural to urban areas and 400 billion square feet of construction under way in the next twenty years, green buildings seem like an obvious solution. Green buildings use renewable energy, such as electricity from concentrated solar power that uses mirrors to intensify the energy from sunlight, and have rainwater recycling and waste reduction systems.

The U.S. nongovernmental organization Natural Resources Defense Council (NRDC) has been working in China for decades, helping the Chinese government formulate environmental policies. Its work spans from energy efficiency to clean power to green buildings to environmental public participation.

"The good news is that China's green engine has started," declared Jin Ruidong, director of the green buildings program at NRDC. "The bad news is, though, China is like a large and heavy train that will take time to gain momentum."[136]

In 2006, the government issued a green building standard and mandated all new construction had to be 50 percent more energy efficient. Some cities like Beijing and Shanghai have to be 60 percent more energy efficient. Simply implementing available technologies such as high-insulation building shells, compact fluorescent lighting, and high-efficiency water heating would cut residential energy growth by more than half.[137]

In addition, innovation and new technologies have emerged for constructing eco-friendly towns and cities that do not drain resources out of the earth. China has the opportunity to leapfrog old, inefficient technologies and introduce cutting-edge technologies at this stage of its production of residential buildings.

To see how these new technologies are affecting Chinese residential development, I visited Chongqing Tiandi, a new development by Shui On Land. Spanning 13.8 million square feet, Chongqing Tiandi is a new community set along the beautiful Jialing River, about a twenty-minute drive from downtown Chongqing. Designed as a green, eco-friendly community, it uses water-source heat pump technology, which takes the warm and cold energy from the earth and exchanges it to heat or cool the buildings. It also has a rainwater recycling system, a green roof system, and water-saving devices.

According to David Nieh, Harvard-educated architect and general manager at Shui On Land, Chongqing Tiandi is LEED Gold certified by the U.S. Green Building Council. "There are three key cycles," David said, "the energy cycle, water cycle, and waste cycle. Up until now, many people considered these to be separate. But if you link them, each one of them has more power. For example, take green waste: a leaf falls and decomposes. If it can be turned into energy, that energy can pump the water to irrigate the trees. The technologies to do this exist."[138]

Frank Yuan, the sales manager of Chongqing Tiandi, showed me their new residential complex along the Jialing River. The new apartment buildings had lofty hall entries with modern décor. They were equipped with swimming pools and tennis courts and surrounded by beautiful landscaping. Many units had breathtaking views of the river. Like Shanghai Xintiandi, the development is designed to preserve local culture and tradition while incorporating modern lifestyle features such as restaurants, coffee shops, and boutique stores. It also has an entertainment complex with movie theaters and an ecological park with a man-made lake. I felt tempted to buy a unit on the spot, as the price was much lower than comparable units in Shanghai and Beijing.

Despite the government mandate, not all green building standards are implemented rigorously. Since China has a central-government-controlled system, policy enforcement is weak at the local level. Wang Miansheng, managing director at the China-U.S. Center for Sustainable Development, told me that some developers took projects and then did whatever they wanted anyway, regardless of energy requirements, because there was no local enforcement.[139]

"There are a lot of green standards in China," Rob Watson said. "But actually the local standards are very flexible and don't mean much. China doesn't yet have the green supply chain of parts, materials, and knowledge needed."[140]

Nonetheless, there is enormous potential for improving energy efficiency using existing technologies in both the United States and China. There are opportunities across the spectrum, from better residential insulation to efficient water heaters, low-energy lighting, and more efficient power generation and transmission.

In the United States, 47 percent of energy use is for electricity and heating. Solar power is an area that needs both economies of scale and technology breakthroughs. Concentrated solar power that uses mirrors to intensify the energy from sunlight can heat fluids to a temperature of up to 400 degrees centigrade. The steam produced can drive turbine generators to create electric power. It could generate up to 22 percent of total power, reduce annual CO_2 emissions by 1.7 gigatons, and generate over five hundred thousand jobs in both China and the United States. However, unless the United States and China make a joint effort, such as massive investments and subsidies, in the near term, concentrated solar power may not even have a future.

The 2010 World Expo in Shanghai, China, showcased a cluster of intelligent green buildings that represent the architectural trends of the twenty-first century. China Pavilion, shaped as an inverted ancient Chinese corbel basket, has an expanding layer-by-layer roof, which provides shade for the entire building and courtyard below. The building incorporates many advanced solar technologies, combined with a large amount of natural ventilation. The roof has eco-friendly gardens where the landscape works as an effective heat insulation layer. Rainwater collected on the roof can be recycled through a sophisticated water filtration system.

Other World Expo green building examples include six "Sun Valley" buildings. A circular glass curtain covering each structure allows the sunshine to pour into an underground garden and collects rainwater for irrigation. Theme Pavilion, another startling green landmark featuring the world's largest "eco-walls," has China's largest single solar roof, which generates electricity for all the pavilions through the municipal power grid.

Imagine what the world would be like if buildings in the future produce more energy and clean water than they use. From solar panels that produce power to tree-filled terraces that recycle water, the building is itself like a living ecosystem where waste becomes nutrition to rebuild soil for plants or generates fertilizer and biogas for cooking. Such a vision is within our reach. Plenty of evidence has shown that by simply applying green technologies, we can clean up our mess on Earth and remake our world based on nature's interdependent cycles, where sustainability and prosperity go hand in hand.

Opportunities for Western Companies

There are plenty of opportunities for Western companies in China's soaring clean-tech industry. Solar panels and smart grids are the fields that look particularly promising for Western companies to get their feet in the door.

As the Chinese middle class demands more electricity and cars, many analysts predict that China will produce two-thirds of the world's solar panels by the end of 2010.[141] Applied Materials, a Silicon Valley-based company, has set up its latest solar research labs in Xi'an, a city in northwest China. Many smaller clean-energy companies are also heading to China. NatCore Technology of Red Bank, New Jersey, developed a technology to make solar panels much thinner, reducing the energy and toxic materials required to manufacture them. The company struck a deal with a consortium of Chinese companies to manufacture the product in large scale.

Smart grids are also beginning to take hold in China. According to *China Daily*, China's state-owned State Grid Corporation plans to invest $586 million constructing smart grids that incorporate wind and solar energy, energy storage, energy transmission monitoring, intelligent substations, and smart meters.[142] Over the next ten years, China will spend more than $100 billion upgrading its power distribution system.[143]

Many Western companies are taking the lead on smart grid technology, and should get a sizable chunk of early contracts from the smart grid market. In May 2010, Siemens struck a deal with Chinese energy management company Wasion Group to conduct feasibility studies in an effort to launch new smart grid pilot projects in China. IBM has launched its Energy and Utility Solutions Lab in Beijing, and is investing heavily in China's smart grid future. IBM expects the China revenues of its energy and utilities division to grow by $400 million from 2010 until 2014. GE announced that it would be partnering with the City of Yangzhou to build a smart grid demonstration center. The goal is to deploy some of the tested technologies within four years. Cisco, Accenture, Hewlett-Packard, ABB, Westinghouse, and Oracle are also vying for a piece of China's smart grid boom.

Other technologies that can be added into the mix include wind power, nuclear power, and carbon capture and storage. Energy efficiency is another area of opportunity. Many existing technologies can already be leveraged, but new technologies will play key roles in our clean, green future. These technologies need to flow across borders, so that they can benefit all, while the rights to those technologies are protected. Intellectual property protection encourages private businesses to invest the large sums required to develop the necessary advanced, costly technologies. International intellectual property protection will require additional attention, especially in China, whose record is weak.

To create the breakthroughs, we will need visionary investors, inventors, and business leaders following an entrepreneurial development model, supported by friendly government policies on both sides of the Pacific. The quality of life and economies of both countries will benefit.

Opportunities for US-China Collaboration

The United States and China are the two largest energy users and greenhouse gas emitters, accounting for more than 40 percent of worldwide emissions each year. China relies on coal for 70 percent of its power, the United States for about 50 percent. Emissions in both countries have continued to increase. These challenges present an opportunity for the United States and China, the two largest polluters, to work together in addressing global environmental crises.

As Brookings fellow Kenneth Lieberthal pointed out, the United States and China have very complementary sets of technologies and engineering capabilities.[144] The United States has state-of-the-art capabilities in wind, solar, biomass, and geothermal. It also has a lead in terms of basic research, human capital, and the ability to move breakthroughs from research to commercialization. China is the world's leading manufacturer of solar panels, the world's largest market for solar hot water heating systems, and one of the world's leaders in the rate at which it is installing wind power plants. China is also pushing rapidly into geothermal heat pumps, and is now fourth in the world in installed capacity.[145] If the two countries work together in developing new clean-energy technologies such as solar power and electric vehicles, they can develop them on a large scale and achieve a major leap in clean energy that neither could make alone.

A good example this kind of collaboration is the work by a small but high impact non-profit organization JUCCCE – Joint US-China Collaboration on Clean Energy. Founded in 2007, JUCCCE aims to accelerate greening China while building trust and cooperation between the U.S. and China. One of JUCCCE's first projects is "Energy Smart Cities Initiative," a series of training sessions for mayors and state-owned enterprise executives across China by leveraging international expertise in clean energy. Such training has proved to play an important role in helping governments and business leaders implement environmental policies. JUCCCE has been instrumental in pushing China to adopt Smart Grid and helped launch China's first Smart Grid business hub. Its founder Peggy Liu was hailed by *Time Magazine* as a Hero of the Environment in 2008.

JUCCCE's latest project, China Dream, is an innovative program designed to decouple rising consumption from rising energy use in China. The team of the China Dream project at JUCCCE not only works with government officials to implement green policies, but also works with industry, advertising agencies, celebrities and trend setters to redefine status symbols for aspiring new Chinese consumers – symbols that are more sustainable and environmentally friendly than "the American Dream." To date, JUCCCE has worked with the Chinese press to create a green consumer tipping point, and trained actress Li Bingbing, singer Cheng Lin, and supermodel Du Juan on green advocacy.

Unfortunately, there is serious mistrust between the United States and China, as reflected in the disastrous Copenhagen outcome. In the United States, there is concern that increased Chinese emissions render meaningless any emission reductions within the United States. Some Americans are concerned that efforts to control emissions within the United States will cause manufacturers to shift operations elsewhere, leading to widespread job loss. On the other hand, many Chinese officials believe that the United States wants to slow down or stop China's rise, and that the United States and other advanced economies use climate change as an excuse to put an extra burden on China and to divide the developing countries.

However, JUCCCE's work provides an excellent model at grassroots level for the United States and China to collaborate and make a joint effort to combat global environmental crises. This will also help build trust between the two countries. Otherwise, we may face serious consequences.

Glittering Memories

Chongqing is a city that grew on me. By the time I was about to leave, I became very fond of it. It is futuristic, dynamic, and ancient all wrapped up in one place. I particularly enjoyed walking along the river, roaming in the old town, and watching the skyline in the mist on both sides of the river.

The night before I left Chongqing, I had dinner with Tang Man-chung, the renowned bridge architect who designed the new Bay Bridge in San Francisco and many other bridges around the world. Mr. Tang divides his time between New York, San Francisco, and Chongqing. His firm in Chongqing has grown rapidly as the city has built some three thousand bridges in recent years. Recently, the firm has started to take on many environmental projects. When I asked about the air pollution in Chongqing, Mr. Tang said, "The haze is not pollution. It is mist from the rivers." He told me that Chongqing has the country's largest natural gas pipeline. All the taxis in Chongqing use natural gas instead of oil. In 2008, Chongqing had forty-six natural gas stations operating in the city to fuel its eight thousand taxis.

It is encouraging to know that the environmental movement in China is on the rise. There are approximately two thousand environmental groups officially registered as nongovernmental organizations (NGOs), with perhaps as many registered as for-profit business entities or not registered at all. At present, China's environmental activists are, in many cases, members of the middle class.

After dinner, Mr. Tang took me for a stroll along the Yangtze River. It started to rain lightly, but we continued our walk despite the rain. The view along the river was spectacular even though half of the skyscrapers were unlit to save energy. At the Chao Tian Men square—the point where the Yangtze River and the Jialing River meet—neon lights were glittering, men and women, mostly in their forties and fifties, were dancing, and occasionally, you could hear the whistling sound of the ships that were slipping in and out of port.

Although grey-haired, Mr. Tang felt invigorated by the breathtaking changes he had seen in Chongqing. "During the New Year," he said, "fireworks and the skyline lit in a dazzling rainbow of lights were reflected in the two rivers. There is no other place like this in the world. You must come back."[146]

I plan to go back to Chongqing someday soon.

Oneness in Environment: Humanity's Common Future

While the threat of global warming and environmental degradation have put planet Earth at serious risk, enormous opportunities exist for the United States and China to cooperate in developing new technologies, creating green jobs, and fighting climate change. Since greenhouse gas emissions threaten the entire planet, a common approach across different countries is essential.

In recent years, both countries have taken significant steps to reduce greenhouse gas emissions. In the United States, green initiatives are a bottom-up movement. For example, more than eight hundred U.S. mayors from all fifty states have pledged that their cities will meet or exceed the Kyoto emissions targets. As the federal government faced significant hurdles to pass a clean energy bill, California went ahead to enact legislation establishing a statewide cap-and-trade program for greenhouse gases. A cap-and-trade program uses economic incentives to reduce emissions.[147] Many other states also launched a mandatory cap-and-trade program for carbon dioxide. State governments have played an important role in promoting renewable energy and energy efficiency in the United States.

In China, reducing pollution operates in a top-down manner. China has very serious clean energy legislation on the books, such as targeting a 20 percent reduction in energy intensity for all GDP in the eleventh five-year plan (2006-2010), increasing the percentage of renewable fuels in China's total energy consumption to 15 percent by 2020, and taking serious measures to reduce emissions from highly polluting power plants. However, implementation of these policies at the local level is typically weak. In addition, coal retains a central role in China's energy mix. The major impetus for most of China's energy policies are to reduce energy consumption, increase efficiency, and expand the use of renewable energy in order to improve energy security and reduce pollution rather than fight global warming.

Both bottom-up and top-down approaches are needed in order to fight global warming. In this regard, the West and China can learn from each other.

If the United States and China can find common ground to work together on important global issues, trust between the two countries will increase. Jointly addressing the challenge of the global environment and climate change goes to, and even goes beyond, the best interests of each country. The United States and China are both at a turning point in determining how to best position themselves to meet the challenges of the twenty-first century and in deciding whether they should join hands to lead the world to a brighter future. If that happens, the world will be a much better place for all.

CHAPTER 6

Democracy or Not Democracy, That Is the Question

"It has been said that democracy is the worst form of government except all the others that have been tried."

– WINSTON CHURCHILL

❧

On a flight between Shanghai and San Francisco, Wang Jun (his name is changed to protect his identity), director of a U.S. corporation's Shanghai R&D center, sat right next to me. In our conversation, I learned Wang was a Beijing native and former Tiananmen Square protestor. Knowing that I was writing a book about the Chinese middle class, our conversation naturally turned to the hottest topic, democracy.

Many people asked me if the Chinese middle class would try to take more control of their government and ask for more democracy. Following the historical examples of the West, it is logical that the Chinese middle class would be a strong force in establishing democracy in China. Meeting Wang Jun gave me an excellent opportunity to explore this topic in depth.

Wang was a college student in 1989 and participated in pro-democracy protests at Tiananmen Square from the beginning to the end (April 21 to June 4). He witnessed the bloodshed in the darkest night before June 4, 1989, and nearly lost his own life.

Wang hinted that after the crackdown, he was detained and interrogated by police. He was forced to write a confession letter to admit that he was wrong in order not to be sent to jail. I understand that many people who participated in the Tiananmen Square demonstration were forced to castigate themselves, a technique widely used by the authorities during the Cultural Revolution.

Shortly after Wang was released, he watched a TV program in which former U.S. President Jimmy Carter visited a village in Jiling province in northern China to observe a village election. Since the 1980s, the Chinese government has organized direct elections of villager committees (VC) for more than six hundred thousand villages across China.[148] At first, it was an experimental program designed to teach China's then eight hundred million peasants their rights and responsibilities by electing their own leaders. In 1987, the National People's Congress passed a provisional law for VC elections, which was made permanent in 1998 after a decade's experiment.

"Most villagers were illiterate," Wang Jun said, "and could not even read candidates' names. The way they elected their village committees was by throwing beans into the bowl in front of each candidate. After I watched the program, I realized that for China to have a meaningful democracy, it would take two more generations. Ignorance was the problem."[149]

Since then, Wang Jun became disillusioned with his quest for democracy. After years of delay, he received permission from the authorities to leave China to study overseas. In 1993, he came to the United States. After earning his Ph.D., Wang worked at a major U.S. technology company.

China has changed dramatically since the Tiananmen Square student demonstration in 1989. Is China now ready for democracy? What is the role of the Chinese middle class in establishing democracy in China? Or is Western democracy a good fit in China's situation?

"Adhere to the Party's basic line unswervingly for 100 years"

To answer these questions, I traveled to Guangzhou, the capital of Guangdong province. Over one thousand miles south of Beijing, Guangzhou has always had a more relaxed political atmosphere. As a Chinese aphorism goes, "the mountains are high and the emperor is far." Because of its geographic proximity to Hong Kong and history of commercial activities, Guangzhou has a distinctive culture that is far different from Beijing and other parts of China. It is more pro-business and less bureaucratic.

My hotel was located in the city center not far from the Pearl River. A beautiful park, named Liu Hua Park, was located next to the hotel. At its entrance, amidst carefully manicured flower beds, a gigantic billboard depicted Deng Xiao Ping standing against a background of new high-rises in the neighboring city of Shenzhen. The billboard was built to commemorate Deng's phenomenal southern tour in 1992, where he decisively set the country on a path towards a market economy. He gave many speeches and urged people to focus on practical matters, such as economic development, rather than ideology. "It doesn't matter if it is a black cat or a white cat," Deng said. "As long as it can catch mice, it's a good cat." He gained large public support from practical-minded southerners who cared little about ideology. His catchphrase, "To Get Rich Is Glorious," unleashed a wave of entrepreneurship that continues to drive China's economy today.

While most people in the West know Deng Xiao Ping as the mastermind behind China's economic reforms, few realize that the man who set the country on the path of a market economy also prescribed a political system that seems incompatible with the underlying principles of the free market. The sign on the billboard states Deng's other catchphrase: "Adhere to the

ic line (meaning reform and opening under one-party
ervingly for 100 years." That means that Deng Xiao
ed the Communist Party as a single party to rule over
China for at least another hundred years. While in Guangzhou,
I picked up a copy of the magazine *South Wind View*. I have long
heard about this outspoken magazine and how it often challenges authority in China. As I flipped through the pages of the
magazine, I was surprised to read: "Fifteen years ago when China
was at a crossroads, a powerful figure led China on the road to
a market economy. He left an important political will: 'Adhere
to the Party's basic line unswervingly for 100 years'...Fifteen
years later, China has reached a point where the original mode of
development seems to have reached its limit. The tide of history,
like the eastern-flowing Yangtze River, seems to flow in circles.
However, it is believed that all the rivers will eventually flow
into the sea."[150]

This is a perfect example of the subtlety and obscurity in the
Chinese language. Any Chinese can read between the lines as follows: "a powerful figure" refers to Deng Xiao Ping, and "original
mode of development" refers to one-party rule that "seems to
have reached its limit." The passage implies that the trend of
democracy is like the Yangtze River flowing east that is unstoppable and will eventually join the ocean. It conveys the message for democratic reform without actually saying it literally.
The obscure language is intentional. In case the magazine is cen-
sored by the government, it cannot be accused of violating any
censorship rules. The same issue of the magazine also contained
an editorial that subtly addressed the question of reforming the
political system, written by the magazine's editor-in-chief, Zhu
Xuedong.

I decided to use my limited stay in Guangzhou to talk to Mr.
Zhu. I jotted down the phone number and called *South Wind View*.
To my surprise, I got through to Mr. Zhu and was immediately
granted an interview for that afternoon.

A Long-delayed Chinese Dream

On my way to *South Wind View*, I stopped by at the Memorial Hall of Dr. Sun Yet-Sen, a great revolutionary forerunner who is revered by people in both mainland China and Taiwan as the founding father of modern China. About one hundred years ago, Sun was instrumental in overthrowing China's five-thousand-year-old imperial system, and he fought all his life for a modern and democratic China.

The memorial hall, surrounded by fifteen acres of green lawns, is an oasis in the midst of the hustling and bustling city. A statue of Dr. Sun Yet-Sen, with one hand on his walking stick and another resting on his waist, stands loftily against the backdrop of the memorial hall built in the Chinese traditional style. The octagonal building is ornamented by a sapphire-blue glaze tile-covered roof, red columns, and white-yellow brick walls. The main hall, almost 22,000 square feet in size, was built without a single interior pillar. Below the brim of the central gate of the hall, a horizontal board was inscribed with Dr. Sun's famous motto: "Justice for All under Heaven."

Sun was born in 1866 to a farmer's family outside of Guangzhou. Some of Sun's family members had emigrated to the United States during the nineteenth century. Two had died in the California gold rush; others had settled in Hawaii. At the age of thirteen, Sun joined an elder brother, Sun Mei, in Hawaii and received an education in the mission schools. In America, Sun was exposed to ideas about democracy as well as Christianity. Later, Sun went to Hong Kong to study Western medicine.

By the end of the nineteenth century, China was on the verge of collapse. Internally, massive social strife threatened the stability of the Qing Dynasty. The Taiping Rebellion (1850-1864) was the first major unrest against the Qing rulers. In the years to follow, countless riots erupted throughout the country. Externally, China suffered from wars with Great Britain, France, and Japan. When Lord McCartney's request to the emperor of Qing to open Chinese markets to British goods was rejected, the United Kingdom declared war on China (the First Opium War). In the following decades between the mid nineteenth and early twentieth centuries, France, Portugal, and Japan fought wars with China and forced it to sign a series of unequal treaties.

As a young man, Sun was deeply troubled by China's backward feudalist system and corrupt Qing government. In 1894, Sun formed the Revive China Society in Hawaii, with the intention of establishing a democratic government against the Qing. After raising some money from his brother and other friends, Sun went to Hong Kong to carry out his revolutionary activities. However, due to the Qing government's arrest warrant for him, Sun fled to Japan, and eventually to San Francisco and London. It was in London where he began to read widely on Western political and economic theories, in search of a recipe to save declining China.

Sun found support among young Chinese who felt little allegiance to the imperial Qing government. In 1905, Sun rallied with other anti-Qing groups and founded the Revolutionary Alliance (which later became the Kuomintang, or Nationalist Party), and pledged to overthrow the Qing government. Between 1906 and 1908, the Revolutionary Alliance directed several uprisings against the government. Even though each uprising was suppressed by the Qing regime, Sun Yet-sen became an inspiring figure to many Chinese. His Revolutionary Alliance gained strong support from the masses.

On October 9, 1911, a military uprising broke out in Wuchang, a city in central China. The uprising led to the collapse of the Qing Dynasty. Sun was in America at the time. He returned to China and was elected to be the "provisional president" of the Republic of China. On January 1, 1912, Sun assumed office in Nanjing, inaugurating the new republic. Hence began China's ill-fated quest for democracy.

Since Sun and his cabinet had no military power, the country soon fell into the hands of warlords. Many provinces declared independence. In exchange for national unity, Sun yielded to military commander Yuan Shi-kai, who controlled the largest army, the Northern Army. Yuan had been patronized by the empress dowager Cixi, a powerful figure who became the de facto ruler of the Qing Dynasty from 1861 to her death in 1908. Yuan was more interested in his personal ambition than Sun's revolutionary ideal. As soon as he assumed power, Yuan restored the old imperial system and appointed himself as the new emperor.

With his dream of democracy ruined, Sun fled to Japan and called for the overthrow of Yuan, which ended in a disastrous failure as Yuan's army easily crushed the remnants of the Kuomintang forces. Yuan's new monarchy, however, survived for only twenty-one days due to strong opposition from the public, mass protests, and military rebellions in different provinces. China then divided into a chaotic civil war of the warlords without a proper central government.

At this stage, many Chinese intellectuals feared that China as a nation would cease to exist. They began to examine a variety of political theories from the West. Some of the country's brightest minds were drawn to Marxist socialism.

By then, Sun realized that control of the military was the key to any vision of a unified, democratic China. In 1917, Sun started an independent southern government in Guangzhou. Although Sun's Nationalist Party enjoyed wider prestige, the Communists were able to organize the working class and peasants to carry out effective strikes. Thus, an alliance between the Nationalists and Communists was born out of a shared hope to unify the fragmented country. Over the next several years, Sun embarked on his Northern Expedition, a military campaign to fight northern-based warlords in an effort to unify the country. That dream, however, was never realized due to his untimely death in 1925.[151]

One of Sun's major legacies was his political philosophy, the Three Principles of the People (sometimes translated as "national sovereignty, democracy, and the people's livelihood"). Sun often said that Abraham Lincoln's Gettysburg Address, "government of the people, by the people, for the people," had been the inspiration for the Three Principles.

How China Has Changed

Since Dr. Sun Yet-sen's time, China has changed a lot, and is still changing. In the past thirty years, China has gradually moved toward the rule of law, albeit under one-party rule. Xu Zhen-xiao, a senior researcher at the Zhejiang Academy of Social Science with a law degree from Xiamen University, gave me a brief history of China's legal system reform.

In 1979, China restored the legal system that was abolished during the Cultural Revolution. At that time, few people were engaged in the legal profession. Most of them were retired academics around sixty years old. A new generation of lawyers, fewer than two hundred people, were still in their sophomore year in college. "They are considered the first generation of lawyers in China," Xu said. "All the lawyers at that time worked for government bureaus and state-owned legal institutes, and they were considered government cadres. The government assigned them jobs and paid their salaries."

In 1988, China had the first bar exam for lawyers. Xu prided himself on being among the first cohorts of lawyers who passed the bar exam. "It was a very difficult and demanding exam," he said. "Only seven out of a thousand people passed the exam." Two years later, in 1990, China started to reform its legal system. Private law firms were allowed to coexist with the state legal institutes. Most legal disputes were limited to commercial cases during this period. Some private business people could go to private law firms to file lawsuits. "But since the state legal institutes had been around for a long time," Xu said, "they already had their clients, like the state-owned enterprises. The private law firms were really disadvantaged."

In 1996, law practice was separated from the state, and all the legal institutes became private. "This changed the nature of the law profession," Xu said. "The duty of lawyers was now to serve society, not the government. Some people began to speak up." Since 1999, the business of private law firms really took off.

"These are the third-generation lawyers in China," Xu said. "The Chinese lawyers charge a very low rate, such as 200 yuan ($30) per hour, compared with U.S. lawyers who charge $600 per hour." In many cases, the pay was not based on hours, but a fixed fee.

"Now, the government has no role in law practice," Xu said. "If the government violates people's rights, people can sue the government. If the government wants to convict somebody, say, issue a fine or revoke a business license, it needs to go through public hearings."[152] It is plausible that China has made significant progress in moving toward the rule of law.

However, since China has one-party rule, the Communist Party is still "all powerful," and often arbitrarily orders investigations and detains dissidents. Deng Feng, a successful entrepreneur in Silicon Valley who returned to China as a venture capitalist, once told me, "If looking at China now, I am not happy with its level of democracy; but if looking at China from a growth perspective, I am happy with where it is, as China is making progress in this regard. Today is better than yesterday, and this year is better than five years ago."[153]

Since 2000, a grassroots rights movement has appeared in China. A new generation of Chinese lawyers has begun to bring court cases against the abuse of power by local officials. Some are active in environmental cases, representing local communities affected by environmental degradation. Others are taking up cases in property-law disputes. As home ownership has increased, there have been many conflicts between new middle class homeowners and property developers and local governments. The number of court cases increased from eight hundred thousand in 1980 to more than ten million in 2008.[154]

Democracy and the Middle Class

I arrived at the office of *South Wind View* on the east side of the city. Although early in May, Guangzhou was already hot and humid. Zhu received me in his office, where stacks of papers, books, and magazines were piled up mountain high. A middle-aged man who appeared deep and wistful, Zhu was intrigued by my book *The Chinese Dream*. Chinese intellectuals are an idealistic type. They tend to be concerned for the fate of the country and become sentimental and mesmerized when it comes to a subject such as "the Chinese dream." I believe that was the main reason why Mr. Zhu agreed to talk to me without hesitation.

In contrast to the style in which he wrote in the magazine, Zhu spoke in a straightforward manner. "China is copying the American model," he said. "The Chinese Dream is a copy of the American Dream." Clearly, Zhu was critical about the commercial activities that had become so prevalent in China in recent years. "The Chinese have become more materialistic than Americans," he said. "But they enjoy fewer protections of rights than Americans—that's all."

"So, do you think the Chinese middle class will ask for more rights and push for democracy?" I was straightforward with him, too.

Holding his cup of tea, Zhu looked me in the eye and said: "The Chinese middle class is still a small percentage of the entire Chinese population. At this stage, they are more a target of multinationals who want to tap into the potentially enormous market than a strong force to push for democracy."[155]

Since the middle class in China is a relatively new phenomenon and is still emerging, they do not yet have the same influence in the country's policymaking as middle class Westerners. They are all busy trying to keep up with the swirling changes happening in China. Most of them approve of what the government has done and enjoy their newfound economic freedom. Geng Hui, an interior designer in Beijing, told me that he couldn't care less about democracy. "I have all the freedom to do the things I want," he said, "and I have more opportunities than I can pay attention to."[156]

In addition, many are happy with where they are in life, as their personal situations have improved dramatically in recent years. In a Pew Global Attitudes Survey, 72 percent of Chinese citizens expressed satisfaction with the way things were going at home, compared with only 39 percent of Americans who were satisfied with conditions in the United States.[157] They see partisanship in Washington, D. C., and not all of them are impressed with Western democracy. Curtis Chin, the gay manager for a shoe company featured in chapter 2, said that he was very content with his income level and living conditions. He was more interested in having a better life rather than fighting for some ideals.

The truth is that the Chinese middle class and the Chinese government want the same thing—continuing economic growth and stability of the country. They prefer to keep the status quo and avoid any radical changes. Some middle class Chinese told me that they wished that their rights were better protected, but they also feel the government is changing and becoming more open. They understand that China is a big country and it has a lot of complex problems. Most importantly, they do not want to lose stability and national sovereignty. When it comes to choosing one, they would choose stability over democracy because middle class Chinese are also beneficiaries of the reform.

He Jie, a businessman who runs a small trading company of industrial equipment in Wuhan, told me that his biggest concern is a change in political system. Referring to Maslow's hierarchy of needs,[158] he said, "In today's China, people just got beyond their physiological needs, such as food and clothing. Now they need to feel secure in their family, health, and property."[159]

He Jie felt that he didn't have a sense of security. He didn't know whether his money in the bank would still be worth the same amount if there was a change in the government. Lighting his cigarette, He Jie examined me from behind his glasses, and said: "For average people, our biggest dream is feeling secure." I could tell that He Jie was not a fan of the Communist Party, as he complained about corruption and a lack of the rule of law in China. Yet, he would rather keep the status quo for fear of losing his business and property.

Throughout my conversation with Mr. Zhu of *South Wind View*, he had remained distant and detached. While straightforward, he was also guarded and made sure everything he said was "politically correct." I asked him about the editorial article he wrote, in which he implied the need for political reform. Zhu admitted that it was not easy to run a magazine that often discussed sensitive topics. "The government has strict guidelines as to what can and cannot be said in the Chinese media," he said. "But it is precisely because we are not satisfied with the current level of democracy (that) we are working to change the system."

Zhu was a member of the Communist Party, which did not surprise me. The government would not let a nonparty member hold an important position in the media. However, being a member of the Communist Party does not mean anything, as I know many liberal-minded party members are also pro-democracy.

"Think about newspapers and magazines ten years ago," Zhu said. "Now we have a lot more freedom." Newspapers and magazines can now criticize the government, corruption, pollution, and so on as long as they do not touch sensitive topics such as overthrowing the Communist Party, separating Tibet, or the Tiananmen Square pro-democracy protests. "It's possible China will change for the better, with more recognition of human rights." Zhu continued. "In the long run, the Chinese middle class will have more voice in how to run the country."[160]

China's Hierarchical Culture

When it comes to democracy, we must not forget that China has come a long way and emerged from a feudal society that lasted for thousands of years.

Dominated by Confucius's (551-479 BC) teaching, China has a long tradition that values hierarchical social order and emphasizes the importance of top-down, rather than bottom-up, governance. Confucianism lays great emphasis on the importance of specific social orders, such as those between the rulers and the ruled, parents and children, and the mutual obligations that these relationships entail. It has enormously influenced Chinese attitudes towards political life and standards of social value. Even today, newspapers call government officials *fumuguan*, or parental officials, which implies they are held in reverence and that their role is to take care of people rather than to be public servants doing their job. It will take time for the concept of democracy to sink in.

Democracy is also linked to economic well-being. In his book *Future of Freedom*, Fareed Zakaria wrote that "when countries become democratic at low levels of development their democracy usually dies."[161] Journalist Robert Kaplan also pointed out that premature enforcement of democracy in countries with rampant poverty led to "widespread violence or authoritarianism."[162] Although the Chinese middle class was about three hundred million strong at the time this book is written, it was still about 23 percent of China's entire population. I can see that in today's China, where the majority of the population are still peasants, if a democracy came into being, most likely it would be abused by organized minorities—powerful castes, rich businessmen, and local thugs—rather than reflecting the will of the majority.

Democracy is like a seed. It needs the right soil in order to grow. Otherwise it may die of malnutrition before it has a chance to bear fruit. A friend of mine, Jose Arocha, who is an activist and social entrepreneur from Venezuela, said insightfully, "Democracy doesn't come from change in the government or revolution. It comes with the silent transformation when people internalize the concept." Even America, founded on the principle of democracy, took a long time to fully achieve it. Its system of slavery persisted for many years, and women could not vote until the twentieth century.

Evidence from other countries, such as South Korea and Taiwan, suggests that when countries advance economically, they begin to democratize when their middle-income status reaches somewhere between $5,000 and $10,000.[163] If this rule applies to China, it will not be too long before we will see some sort of democracy movement in China.

Viable Opposition

A more important question, perhaps, is to examine whether viable oppositions exist in China that would allow a democracy to blossom.

Since the 1990s, the Communist Party has increased its efforts to recruit new members in private firms and foreign companies. Traditionally, party organizations were strong in the state-owned enterprises. With an exponential increase in the numbers of private firms and foreign companies, the Communist Party was concerned about losing support from young people and started a campaign to recruit new members in private and foreign companies. According to the *Economist,* by the end of 2006, party organizations had been established in more than two-thirds of private enterprises and foreign companies.[164]

While the most competitive young people in America went into business, or even, in recent years, nonprofits, some of the brightest young people in China went into the government and joined the Communist Party. They recognized that the party is the only game in town and that party membership has significant advantages, such as career advancement, social status, or personal connections.

In the television program "China: the Dragon's Ascent" on the History Channel, an ambitious young student at Fudan University—one of the top universities in China—said,

"I really want to do something for the country. I want to join the Communist Party so that I can better serve my country." Another student, who was planning to go overseas to study, said: "If I go abroad, I won't join the party. But if I cannot go overseas, I may join the party." Other students agreed with him that if he stayed in China, he should join the party because of its significant advantages. The Communist Party is adamant about qualifications, such as academic achievements or career credentials. Its new generation of leaders all seem to have postgraduate degrees, often from the United States.

If the best young people have been recruited by the Communist Party, the question is whether China will permit a viable opposition to exist and become a rival of the Communist Party. This is critical, as without opposition, there will be no real democracy.

On December 10, 2008, on the sixtieth anniversary of the United Nations' Universal Declaration of Human Rights, 303 courageous Chinese citizens signed a petition known as "Charter 08," a manifesto for democracy. The charter members challenged the Communist Party's totalitarianism and pointed out that "China has many laws but no rule of law; it has a constitution but no constitutional government." They called for political reform and laid out nineteen recommendations that included overhauling the constitution so that "the constitution must be the highest law in the land, beyond violation by any individual, group, or political party"; separation of legislative, judicial, and executive powers; and systematically implementing general elections of public officials.[165] Charter 08 essentially calls for ending one-party rule.

Such an extraordinary call for democracy went largely unnoticed both inside and outside China. The government reacted quickly and nervously to censor the charter. Liu Xiaobo, a well-known dissident who was the lead signatory, was detained even before the petition was released. Other signatories were summoned or interrogated by police. The document was deleted from the Internet behind China's great firewall. In the past, Chinese Internet-savvy Web surfers were able to get around the firewall without much difficulty to find out the truth if they wanted to. But this time, very few people in China even paid attention. Almost everyone I talked to (even Wang Jun, the former Tiananmen Square demonstrator) said he or she had never heard about Charter 08. Not only that, the foreign media were unusually quiet about it. The *New York Review of Books* published a complete translation of Charter 08 by Perry Link. However, almost none of the overseas Chinese I talked to knew about it, despite the fact that they were on top of everything about China—businesswise. (Postscript: Liu was later sentenced to eleven years in prison for "inciting the subversion of state power." On October 8, 2010, Liu was awarded the Nobel Peace Prize.)

The reason that Charter 08 did not reach its intended effect lies beyond the government's censorship. Although months later, about eight thousand Chinese citizens had signed their names online, the number is much less than 1 percent of China's Internet population. I looked up the original signatories. Most of them were writers, poets, scholars, and lawyers. Even though everything they advocated makes perfect sense, the first question people would ask is, who will be the actual persons to carry out these reforms, and who can actually compete with the Communist Party on every level, from changing constitutions to establishing an adequate social security system? The answer to these questions is, very unfortunately, no one. There are no strong opposition parties in China to make political reform toward democracy a reality.

This is one of the major reasons that the people in China have put up with the Communist Party. They still remember China's history that, when the Qing Dynasty collapsed, there was no capable governance and the country fell into chaos. They do not want China to repeat that history. Many people I talked to expressed the concern that if the Communist Party was not in power, who else could run such a big country with so many complex problems? Wu Xiaoguang, a researcher on the Yangtze River cruise, said to me that "a corrupted government is better than a country that is in chaos or civil wars." The Communist Party has won a lot of legitimacy and credibility for having led China to where it is today.

However, without viable opposition, the ideal for a democratic China remains only a dream by a few enlightened Chinese intellectuals.

A Single Spark Can Start a Prairie Fire

While it seems not very promising at this time, I believe that as China's economy continues to grow and privatize, it is only a matter of time for oppositions to arise. Not all the best young people have joined the Communist Party. Some private entrepreneurs have become active in the Chinese People's Political Consultative Conference (CPPCC), a consultative group of democratic parties in China.

In Beijing, I met with a thirty-three-year-old, ambitious entrepreneur whom I'll call Zhang Wei. Born in a village in Zhejiang province, Zhang went to one of the top universities in China. After graduating from college, he worked as a management trainee in a U.S. multinational corporation in Beijing, and then moved to a state-owned company. In 2005, he founded a mobile social networking company and hoped to take the company to an IPO or merge with a bigger company. A fan of Andrew Carnegie, Zhang is one of those upwardly mobile young Chinese who admire Western democracy. Shortly into our conversation, he openly told me that he is in a democratic party.

"There is a democratic party in China?" I was surprised.

"You don't know?" Zhang said. "There are eight democratic parties in China."

Nominally, China has eight democratic parties under CPPCC. They are in compliance with the Communist Party and serve as a consultative function for the government rather than competitors.

"But these parties are small," I said. "And they are controlled by the Communist Party."

"The party I am in is not that small," Zhang said. "We are growing very fast."

The party Zhang belongs to is called China Democratic National Construction Association (CDNCA). It was founded in 1945, before the Communist Party took power in China. Party members are mainly industrialists and private business owners. In recent years, the members of the party have increased dramatically. Zhang told me that the party had about six hundred thousand members. This compares with the seventy million members in the Communist Party.

"China is actually going on the capitalism road," Zhang said. "I doubt the Communist Party is capable of handling the situation. Corruption is very bad. The main reason for corruption is the communist system. There is no cross-checking function." Zhang is one of the few I met in China who was not afraid to challenge the authorities. He admitted that it was very difficult to abolish the Communist Party, but hinted that there may be a dramatic change in China's political system.

Zhang was very optimistic about China's future even though there are a lot of uncertainties. He liked American culture and loved Hollywood movies. "In the future," he said. "I hope I am rich enough to have money to help poor people and build schools. There are a lot of poor people in rural areas. Although their income has increased, the cost of living has also risen. It's now very expensive to send kids to school."

I asked him why he wanted to join a democratic party. Zhang said, "I feel if one day China's political system changes, democratic parties may have a chance."[166]

I left our meeting feeling in awe. I do not know how many Zhang Weis are out there. Many people in China told me that only when they have economic freedom, they will have political freedom. There is a sense among the Chinese middle class that the trend of democracy is unstoppable. Even a single spark can start a prairie fire.

It is clear that China's political system is ill fitted to address the needs of an increasingly pluralized society. In fact, cracks have already shown in China's seemingly unified leadership. In early 2012, Bo Xilai, the former party secretary of metropolitan Chongqing, was purged after an accusation of "violating the party rule." Son of a revolutionary figure in Mao's time, Bo Xilai is a charismatic politician who was believed to be a contender for China's future top leader. He made his name in Chongqing for his bold initiatives such as cracking down on crime organizations and singing "red songs" (revolutionary anthems from the days of the Cultural Revolution). His fall from grace was linked to the mysterious murder of British businessman Neil Heywood, who was a friend of Bo's family, Heywood was found dead in a Chongqing hotel in November 2011. Bo's police chief, Wang Lijun, reportedly told Bo that his wife, Gu Kailai, a once highflying lawyer, was involved in murdering Mr. Heywood. As a result, Wang was demoted by Bo. Wang later fled to the U.S. consulate in an attempt to seek political asylum for fear of his life. This whole drama prompted an investigation by the central government over Bo and his wife. Bo was soon removed from his post in the Party. His wife Gu Kailai was arrested as a major suspect in Mr. Heywood's death.

Some people in China believe that the real reason for Bo Xilai's downfall is political power struggles. Bo, although considered a political hardliner, was a liberal as mayor of Dalian, governor of Liaoning province, and the Party secretary of Chongqing metropolitan area. Both Dalian and Chongqing were phenomenally transformed from rundown cities to modern metropolises under his tenure. In Chongqing, he pioneered a new model of governance, the so-called "Chongqing Model," that advocated a return to socialism while promoting market-oriented economic growth. His flamboyant style in interacting with the media set him apart from other stern-faced Chinese leaders. For his achievements in Chongqing, Bo was name by *Time Magazine* as one of "the world's 100 most influential people" in 2010. Bo's popularity may have caused resentment from other top Chinese leaders. His "Chongqing Model" was also considered a challenge to the economic model championed by President Hu Jintao and Premier Wen Jiabao. Sources revealed that the central government started to investigate Bo Xilai even before the scandal of his wife's involvement in Mr. Heywood's death.

The story of Bo Xilai's rise and fall signals an ongoing dilemma for China's central government — the lack of systemic political reform. This could present serious challenges for China, now the world's second-largest economy, upon which global growth increasingly depends. Moving forward, I see two possible outcomes: either the Chinese government will gradually be forced into political reform, or change will come more radically because of an economic or political breakdown.

Middle Class Pushes Back

Although the Chinese middle class does not want radical changes, they have started to voice their opinions and show signs of power that never existed before. The Internet and mobile phones have played a significant role in this process.

In an "American Idol"-like "Super Girl's Voice" singing contest, Chinese youth used mobile phones to vote for their favorite singers. The show drew an audience of four hundred million people nationwide. The media covered it like an American presidential campaign. Thousands of young talents competed for votes as well as the spotlight. By the end of the show, twenty-one-year-old Li Yuchun from Sichuan province received eight million votes by text messages and became one of the most popular pop stars in China.[167]

In 2006, Shenzhen's middle class families learned about a highway construction project that would cut through their neighborhood. They organized a campaign requesting the city government to change the plan, and managed to halt construction while negotiating with the city. Eventually, the city government changed the highway route to reduce pollution from the highway in the neighborhood.[168]

In November 2008, China rushed through a 4 trillion yuan ($585 billion) economic stimulus package. People debated vigorously in blogs and online media about how the stimulus plans were organized and what measures were used to supervise the spending. Critics inside and outside the Communist Party pressed for details about the spending and demanded the right to follow the money. A Shanghai-based lawyer, Yan Yiming, filed a lawsuit against the National Development and Reform Commission (NDRC), China's de facto central planning agency, after being ignored in his request to disclose all relevant details of the entire package. Although Yan's suit was rejected by the Beijing High People's Court, a lawsuit against the central government agency was unprecedented. [169]

In May 2009, the Chinese government issued a statement to require all the computers sold in China to preinstall spyware called "Green Dam Youth Escort," effective July 1, 2009. It was pitched as a tool to block pornographic content from personal computers. However, the software was seen as part of the "Great Firewall" to censor the Internet. China's three hundred million Internet users reacted, strongly opposing installation of the software. After weeks of criticism from the public, the Chinese government backed off and later announced that "Green Dam" was no long required to be preinstalled on new computers.[170]

These are just a few examples of how the Chinese middle class has begun pushing back and demanding more protection for their rights, property, and privacy. Incidents like these will no doubt expedite democratic processes in China. And once democracy becomes established, the middle class usually turns into a strong supporter of it.

Where China Is Heading

After our flight took off, Wang Jun, the former Tiananmen Square demonstrator, grabbed a SkyMall shopping magazine and started to flip through it. He pointed to the picture of a HairMax LaserComb, a hair loss treatment device, and said, "I'd like to get this when the price drops a little." Rubbing his skull of thinning hair, Wang continued, "The students' intentions were good. But the result was not. Democracy cannot happen overnight. In order for China to have democracy, I believe it needs a system. I am now working on projects related to netbooks (mini-notebook computers with Web-based applications) which allows more people to access the Internet. I think this is a more effective way to promote democracy."

Wang Jun was pleased with how China had progressed since 1989. He was optimistic about the direction China was going, although he felt progress could be faster. "I think Hu Jintao (China's president) is a very wise person," he said. "I believe he will be the first Chinese leader to speed up democracy. I predict China will have elections within the party in five years, and hopefully have general elections in ten years."

Wang Jun may be too optimistic. On December 18, 2008, Hu Jintao delivered a speech that is seen as a response to Charter 08's call for political reform. Hu Jintao acknowledged that without democracy, the modernization of China could not be achieved. However, he also made it clear that China would never copy the mode of Western political institutions. In March 2009, Wu Banguo, the chairman of China's National People's Congress, issued a tough statement, saying that China would never adopt a system of "multiple parties holding office in rotation, or hold elections without government-chosen candidates on the ballot."

Mr. Wu added, "Without a single Communist Party in control, a nation as large as China would be torn by strife and be incapable of accomplishing anything."[171]

The year 2009 saw regression in the move towards democracy. The government disbarred fifty-three lawyers who were actively involved in civil rights and corruption cases. The office of a prominent lawyers' group, known as Gong Meng, or Open Constitution Initiative, was shut down by the authorities. Its thirty-six-year-old founder, Xu Zhiyong, who has taken on high-profile cases such as the tainted milk scandal, was detained on the charge of tax violation. Some people believe that the real reason for shutting down Gong Meng is Mr. Xu's activism on civil rights.

As Zhu of *South Wind View* wrote, the tide of history, like the eastern-flowing Yangtze River, seems to flow in circles. However, it is believed that all the rivers will eventually flow east into the sea. As Tang Xiaozhao, one of the eight thousand ordinary Chinese who signed Charter 08, was quoted as saying, "I was afraid, but I had already signed it hundreds of times in my heart."[172] I remain hopeful that the day of democracy will come in China. The long-delayed dream of Dr. Sun Yet-Sen for "government of the people, by the people for the people" will eventually come true.

Oneness in Politics: Different Forms of Democracy

I believe that a growing Chinese middle class will eventually help the democratization of China, which is not only crucial for the stability of China, but also for the stability of the world. However, China may adopt a different form of democracy.

While the Chinese are very sophisticated in terms of culture and philosophy, they are less sophisticated in modern institutions such as political, financial, and legal systems. However, for the past three decades, Chinese leaders have been avidly learning from the West, importing enormous amounts of

Western knowledge about business know-how as well as political systems. The Chinese government has sent delegations to Singapore, Japan, and Sweden to study their political systems and electoral rules, trying to understand how those countries have created a democratic polity dominated by a single party. They have also investigated what Norway and other countries have done with their economies.

The United States developed a democratic system that worked out reasonably well for its particular national characteristics. For China, with its long history and hierarchical culture, the answers may work out in a different way. Confucius said, "The highest attainment for a learned person is to become a scholar to serve the imperial government." So enlightened persons can serve the country and lead it to common good. In China, a small group of so-called "elites" has tremendous influence to determine which direction China is going in because of its pro-elite culture.

In northern Europe where social democracy occurs, government takes civil society into itself and guides it and tries to direct it toward some sort of common good. Social scientists have suggested that this type of system and government may be a better fit for China (although evidence suggests that the model is not very successful). My guess is that China may eventually be more like France, where an elite group of officials who have attended the country's *grandes ecoles* commands both the public and private sector.

As the Chinese middle class continues to grow, democracy will arise in its time. The question is whether China can make a peaceful transition to democracy. It is not only important to the Chinese people, but also critical to the West, and to world peace. Oneness in politics implies the possibility of different forms of democracy. A democratic system that fits China's situation may not look the same as the one in the West, and it doesn't have to.

CHAPTER 7

Looking at the World Upside Down

"The ability to learn faster than your competitors
may be the only sustainable competitive advantage."

– ARIE DE GEUS

I n 2004, I returned to Stanford University as an industrial fellow to work on projects that use technology to help underserved communities. After ten years working in start-ups in
Silicon Valley, I felt it was time for me to do something that I
care dearly about and use my skills for the greater good. I was
interested in addressing social problems and finding innovative
solutions that could help transform the system and allow society
to take new leaps.

The project I developed, e-Mobilizer, was to help microentrepreneurs, mostly women, in developing countries to access the
Internet marketplace using their mobile phones. It occurred to
me that the biggest problem facing these microentrepreneurs is
the inability to access the larger public market and its market
information. They do not have efficient channels to reach customers. This disadvantage creates a major obstacle that limits their
potential, and often forces them into a life of poverty. E-Mobilizer
can solve this problem by leveraging the existing cellular infrastructure to connect microentrepreneurs to online markets and

help them to post their products and services so that they can grow their businesses and generate incomes. Just like microcredit gives poor people access to capital, e-Mobilizer gives them access to markets and information.

Being at the intersection of entrepreneurship, technology innovation, and social improvement was both exciting and rewarding. I worked with energetic students, professors, and technologists to develop a prototype. During this period, I traveled back and forth to China extensively to do field work. Our strategy was to work with Internet marketplaces such as eBay and Alibaba, a Chinese e-commerce site. Porter Erisman, a Stanford graduate and vice president of Alibaba at the time, was enthusiastic about our project and supported the collaboration.

It was an exciting time for China as well. Technology start-ups were sprouting up to highlight the already fascinating landscape of the Chinese economy. They ranged from e-commerce sites to video-sharing portals, from Internet search engines to social networking sites. Almost every coastal city has a "technology park" which is modeled after Silicon Valley and incubates new technology ventures. Venture capital firms from the United States and other countries have been racing into China to look for the next new, new thing—although they may soon find out that there are totally different kinds of new, new things in China.

While visiting Alibaba's headquarters in Hangzhou, I felt the same "insanely great" energy of entrepreneurship as I felt in Silicon Valley. In 2004, eBay had just entered China and was planning to dominate the China market. Alibaba was a local Chinese company that helped small- and medium-sized enterprises conducting business online. Most people in the West had barely heard about it. When I asked a senior manager at Alibaba whether the company was worried that it would be bought by eBay, I was blown away by the answer: "We will buy eBay!"

I was fascinated by the rivalry between eBay and Alibaba in China. I used to write columns about entrepreneurship in Silicon

Valley for *Hong Kong Economic Journal* (a *Wall Street Journal* equivalent for Hong Kong). I kept a blog and followed closely as their competition unfolded.

The case of Alibaba defeating eBay in China will be documented in the business schools. Alibaba's Jack Ma represents a new generation of savvy competitors and technocrats in China. They study their markets and bring to bear their local knowledge. They learn from their competition and from their own mistakes as they move up the competitive landscape. The case of Alibaba provides an invaluable lesson for multinationals to succeed in the China market.

Jack Ma: See the World Upside Down

In May 2003, the board room at Alibaba's headquarters in Hangzhou was filled with smoke from cigarettes. The top management team was intensely debating about a life-and-death decision the company was about to make. A young company just four years old, Alibaba was an e-commerce site for small- and medium-sized enterprises conducting business online. Its charismatic chairman and CEO, Jack Ma, proposed to start a sister site, Taobao, to compete with eBay, which had just entered China. The team had always believed in their leader, who was known as an oddity with an unconventional vision. But this time, they were not sure. eBay had everything that Alibaba could not match: it was a multinational with billions of dollars in revenue, whereas Alibaba was a small local company, still struggling with growing pains and barely making any profit. Moreover, eBay had leading-edge technology and a strong international brand with a record of success, not to mention its top-notch management team, who were mostly graduates from Harvard Business School. Alibaba had none of those. It was laughable to even think of the idea. Was Jack Ma really insane?

"Okay, everyone," Jack Ma said, clapping his hands and rolling up his sleeves. "Let's all get up and stand against the wall."

Everyone stood up from their chairs, wondering what sleight of hand their boss would show.

"Now, I want you all to stand on your heads," Jack Ma said.

"What? You want us to stand upside down?" one member of the executive team asked in disbelief.

"Yes, stand upside down on your heads," Jack Ma said.

"Oh, no," another member murmured. "I have never done that in my life, and I am too old for that."

"No excuse," Jack Ma said. "I am the oldest among this group. We'll all stand upside down on our heads."

So, everyone in the room, one by one, managed to stand upside down on his or her head like the headstand pose in yoga practice.

After they finished the exercise, Jack Ma said, "When you stand upside down, you'll see the world from a new perspective." Then he turned to the person who said he had never stood on his head. "You see, you can do things that you have never done before."[173]

Jack Ma continued: "EBay may be famous in the United States, but in China, if you ask one hundred people whether they've heard about eBay, I believe that less than 10 percent have heard of it. But if you ask one hundred people whether they've heard about Alibaba, 90 percent know about us. Although eBay has acquired four million users (via EachNet, the company eBay acquired to enter China), compared with eighty million Internet users in China (at the time), it was still a small penetration. I believe we have a chance."[174]

Thus began one of the most startling competitions between a global giant and a small maverick company.

eBay Comes to China

In the summer of 2003, Meg Whitman, CEO of eBay, was in Shanghai finishing up the final acquisition of EachNet, a Chinese online auction site founded by Harvard graduate Bo Shao in 1999. In March 2002, eBay and EachNet had entered a strategic partnership when eBay purchased 33 percent of EachNet shares for $30 million. In June 2003, eBay acquired the remaining EachNet shares for another $150 million and became sole owner of EachNet.[175] The acquisition was considered a good fit. Most of EachNet's product features were adapted from eBay's. Both companies shared a similar culture inherited from Silicon Valley—upbeat, fun, and full of optimism. Although EachNet had only about four million users, it held a commanding 85 percent market share in China. The acquisition paved the way for eBay to enter the China market, a potentially immense market with hundreds of millions of small businesses selling on the Internet.

Whitman was very excited. The timing was perfect for eBay. China's economy had been growing in double digits for the past two decades. China's Internet users were likely to surpass those in the United States, making China the number one Internet country in the world in terms of users. "Ten to fifteen years from now," Whitman predicted, "China can be eBay's largest market on a global basis as we build up the local trade and export trade."[176] Looking out from EachNet's twenty-fifth-floor office window over Nanjing Road and its shopping malls crammed with shoppers, Whitman was convinced that China was a top priority for eBay's global presence and "is likely to be the defining measure of business success on the Net."

However, one thing had bothered Whitman lately. A new online auction site called Taobao, owned by local company Alibaba, had just launched in May 2003. Jack Ma, a former English teacher who founded Alibaba, started drawing media attention for his suicidal attempt to fight eBay.

Whitman did not consider Taobao a threat. As she told the *Wall Street Journal*, there were many "small competitors nipping at our heels." What troubled her was that Taobao was backed by Masayoshi Son's Softbank, which also backed Yahoo! Japan to

defeat eBay in Japan's market. EBay had closed its Japanese operation one year earlier and retreated from the market. The sting
of losing the Japanese market was still painful. But this time it
would be different. Whitman was determined. "China is a must-
win," she said. "Whoever wins China wins the world."[177]

Jack Ma's Uncharacteristic Path

It was hard to imagine Jack Ma as the man who kept the CEO of
mighty eBay awake at night. At age thirty-nine, he was barely five
feet tall, skinny, and frail, as if he could be easily blown away by the
wind. His boyish haircut made him look younger than his age. His
square forehead and sunken cheeks give him an alien-like look—a
look, according to Chinese face-reading astrology, that suggests some
kind of abnormality in a person's fate. He often wears a big grin that
some people find disarming, while others see it as a disguise. Fluent in
English, he charms Western businessmen with jokes that shine with
Eastern wisdom. People who know him describe him as a "funny
guy" and "genius in a peculiar way." Hardly knowing anything about
technology, Ma started one of the first Internet companies in China.

Ma was born in November 1964 to a family of three children
in Hangzhou. His mother worked in a factory that assembled
clocks and watches; his father ran a dramatic-arts association.
Growing up in the beautiful lakeside city, Ma learned to speak
English by listening to the Voice of America on radio and playing tour guide for foreign tourists. At age thirteen, he started
to hang out at the Hangzhou Hotel (now the Shangri-la Hotel),
located on the north bank of West Lake. It was the only hotel
that accommodated foreign guests at that time. Young Ma offered
free guided tours to English-speaking foreigners, recounting leg-
ends of West Lake, from the history of the Mausoleum of General
Yue Fei to the mythical love story of the White Snake Lady on
the Broken Bridge.[178] Ma offered his guide service for nine years
until he turned twenty-one. The experience polished his English

and prepared him for something later in life that would be much bigger than young Ma could have dreamed of.

After having failed the college entrance exams twice, Ma was finally admitted to the Hangzhou Teachers Institute, where in 1988 he earned a degree in English which was considered neither glamorous nor impressive. After his graduation, Ma taught English for several years at Hangzhou Electronic and Engineering Institute, another lesser-known college. Earning $10 a month as a teacher, Ma seemed destined to lead a simple and ordinary life.

Ma enjoyed working as a teacher—drinking beer and playing cards with colleagues and friends—until something happened that changed his life forever.

In 1995, Ma traveled to the United States for the first time as an interpreter for a joint-venture project. The trip brought him to Malibu, California, a beachfront city about thirty-five miles west of Los Angeles. While there, Ma was trying to collect a debt on behalf of a friend from an American businessman, whom I'll call "Fred." What happened exactly is not clear, but Fred refused to pay back the money he owed. He locked Ma in his house, trying to force Ma to conspire in a deal with him. "At one point," Ma said, "he started playing with his handgun. It was obviously meant as a threat."[179]

Although Malibu was all sunshine and sandy beaches full of bikini-clad women, Ma recalled the western movies he saw back home with cowboys riding their horses and shooting at anyone without blinking an eye. Ma didn't dare to say anything, but complied with whatever Fred asked. At the same time, he was looking for an opportunity to escape.

A few days later, Fred took Ma to Las Vegas, a routine showcase trip for Chinese businessmen visiting America. However, Las Vegas' flashy neon lights and excessive luxuries did not ease Ma's anxiety over being Fred's captive. Although almost penniless by then, he decided to try his luck at gambling. After all, what could he lose? Luck must have been on Ma's side: he won $600 simply by playing the slot machines! With a few hundred dollars in his pocket, Ma bought a plane ticket to Seattle and fled, leaving all his belongings behind at Fred's. "It was a terrible experience," Ma later said. "Every time I think of L.A., I have a nightmare."[180]

Ma's fate took a dramatic turn in Seattle. While visiting a friend there, he noticed a gray box with a screen on the desk in his friend's home. Ma had never seen a computer before. It looked to him like some kind of military device used in the People's Liberation Army.

"What the heck is this?" Ma was a little apprehensive.

"Jack, it's not a bomb," his friend said, "It's a computer. Just touch it and play with it anyway you want."

It was the first time Ma discovered the Internet. He typed in "beer," and it returned a list of results. Then he typed in "beer" and "China," but it yielded nothing. In 1995, Netscape had just started, and Yahoo! was barely launched. Very few people in the United States understood the Internet, and fewer could foresee its future impact. Even fewer people in China knew what it was all about. But Ma sensed a big opportunity—he believed "this Internet thing" was going to change the world. After he returned home, he borrowed $2,000 from friends and family and set up what is believed to be the first commercial Web site in China called "China Pages," a directory service for businesses in China.

The Birth of Alibaba

Ma's first entrepreneurial attempt was a disaster. China Pages was running on a server with a dial-up connection in his apartment in Hangzhou. When he first got connected, it took three and a half hours to load a half page. Ma joked that they could often play a few rounds of poker while waiting for a page to appear. Perhaps those prolonged moments of waiting were a blessing in disguise. "I've learned a lot of business philosophy by playing poker," he said.[181] But not knowing how to monetize this "take-forever-to-load" Web site, he ran out of money pretty quickly. Ma then took a job with the Ministry of Foreign Trade and Economic Cooperation.

However, Ma did not give up. Four years later, in February 1999, Ma managed to raise $60,000 from eighteen friends and launched an e-commerce Web site for small- and medium-sized businesses conducting business online. In a videotaped inaugural meeting at his Hangzhou apartment, Ma spoke with great enthusiasm about his vision: there were hundreds of millions of small- and medium-sized enterprises in Zhejiang province. Ma believed the Internet could connect these small companies, which were mostly privately owned and ignored by government planning.

It was probably the first time Ma displayed his charisma and his sense of humor. He wanted to call his new venture "Alibaba" after Ali Baba, the poor carpenter who accidentally found abundant treasure in the tale in *One Thousand and One Nights*. Since his childhood, Ma had been fascinated by the story of Ali Baba and the Forty Thieves and how an unfortunate woodcutter had adventurously altered his fortune. The story may be fantasy for many people, but not for Ma. He saw the Internet as the abundant treasure hidden inside the magic cave, with Alibaba as the magic door that could be opened to millions of poor carpenters.

Sounds like magic? Maybe. But no one came to knock on the magic door of Alibaba. The small business owners in Zhejiang province were mostly "mom-and-pop shops." Most had no education beyond middle school, if any education at all. Although they had made some money during the economic boom, doing business on the Web was completely foreign to them. Realizing his customers needed to be educated about the Internet, Ma sent troops out to knock on the doors of the mom-and-pop shops, much like door-to-door sales in the United States. In addition, Alibaba provided services that ranged from setting up Internet connections to registering on the Alibaba Web site.

Another problem facing Alibaba was trust. China had no credit checking system, and these small businesses had no credit history.

In a business environment that was very much like the Wild Wild West in the United States a hundred years ago, there were no rules or laws. Cheating and lying were the norm in doing business there. To ensure that people were willing to do business online, Ma and his team built a "trust system" called TrustPass, which perfectly suited China's situation. When people registered on the site, for a small fee Alibaba would hire a third party to verify their business licenses, physical addresses, bank accounts, and so on. This system was a huge help in building e-commerce infrastructure in China.

Six months after Alibaba was launched, Goldman Sachs and a group of venture capital firms invested $5 million in Ma's new venture. Soon after, Masayoshi Son, the founder of Softbank, appeared at his door. Son and his Softbank had invested in more than three hundred Internet companies around the world. His most renowned deals included portals such as Yahoo! Inc., online trading sites such as E*Trade Group, Inc., as well as a variety of e-commerce players in the United States and Asia. Like Ma, Son had plenty of boyish charm and a disarming grin. They hit it off immediately. At the end of the meeting, Son put $20 million into Alibaba and became Ma's biggest backer.

The basic service of Alibaba was free. Profit came from a small percentage of users who paid premium prices that ranged from $5,000 to $10,000 a year for special services such as personalized Web pages and priority listings. In addition, Alibaba flew its top-tier customers to Hangzhou for a two-day conference and training sessions on e-commerce, which taught everything from setting up e-mail accounts to writing polite inquiry letters to basic business etiquette. These efforts paid off handsomely. As a result, Alibaba achieved a 70 percent renewal rate in retaining its paid customers.

"eBay May Be a Shark in the Ocean, But I Am a Crocodile in the Yangtze River"

Ma was happy with his e-commerce niche until eBay bought one-third of EachNet in 2002. Most of Alibaba's customers were small business owners who were buying and selling on Alibaba. When eBay entered the China market, Ma was alarmed that "someday, eBay would come in our direction."[182] He knew too well that there was no clear distinction between small businesses and individual consumers in China. As a defensive strategy, Ma decided to launch a competing consumer-to-consumer (C2C) auction site, not to make money, but to fend off eBay from taking away Alibaba's customers.

In 2004, I visited Alibaba at its headquarters in Hangzhou. It is located on a campus of three ten-story buildings in the north-eastern part of Hangzhou, about a ten-minute taxi drive from West Lake. In the lobby, a flat panel TV was streaming video clips of Jack Ma speaking at various public events where his admirers, most of them in their twenties, were cheering him like a rock star

By then, Ma's empire had grown into three entities: Alibaba International, an online business-to-business (B2B) marketplace with 2.5 million registered users from more than two hundred countries; Alibaba China, a Chinese language business-to-business site with fourteen million registered users focusing on domestic trade; and Taobao, an online consumer-to-consumer (C2C) auction site competing directly with eBay.

"Being in Hangzhou gives us a big advantage in keeping us close to customers and making us think differently," Ma said. "If we were in Beijing or Shanghai, we'd be just another company."[183]

Surely Alibaba was not just another company. To many Chinese young entrepreneurs, Ma was a hero who dared to challenge the global giant eBay. To Ma, confronting eBay was in fact a defensive move at the beginning. He picked a perfect partner in this battle, Masayoshi Son, who had a track record of beating back eBay in Japan with his Yahoo! Japan joint venture. By then, Ma and Son had become good friends. Son had growing faith in Ma: "He's got incredible management ability. If there is a company outside of America that can introduce a new business model to the world, it's Alibaba."[184]

In May 2003, Son's Softbank invested $56 million in Alibaba to bet on Ma's ability to topple eBay in China. A new Web site named Taobao—meaning "digging for treasure"—was launched free of charge for individuals buying and selling virtually any consumer goods, from cosmetics to electronic parts. EBay, on the other hand, began its most aggressive campaigns to dominate the market and thwart competitors. Soon after Taobao was launched, eBay signed exclusive advertising rights with major portals Sina, Sohu, and Netease with the intention of blocking advertisements from Taobao. In addition, eBay injected another $100 million to build its China operation, now renamed "eBay EachNet," and was spreading its ads on buses, subway platforms, and everywhere else.[185]

Ma fought back cleverly. Knowing that most small business people would rather watch TV than log on to the Internet, Ma secured advertisements for Taobao on major TV channels. In 2004, one could easily feel the heat of fierce competition between eBay EachNet and Taobao. When I was taking a taxi in Shanghai, I noticed the ads of eBay EachNet on the back of the driver's seat; when I checked into my hotel, I heard the ads for Taobao popping up on TV almost every half hour. Since its name means "digging for treasure" in Chinese, it attracted a lot of attention by a smart play on words. While most people in the West had never heard of Taobao, its name was heard loud and strong in China.

Nevertheless, most industry observers were suspicious about Taobao's future, particularly its sustainability. Unlike eBay EachNet, which charged its sellers for listing and transaction fees, Taobao was free to use. Neither Ma nor any members from the management team gave a definite timeline as to how long this "free period" was going to last. "Free is not a business model," sniffed the competitors and doubters. Some thought Ma was crazy and nicknamed him "Crazy Ma."

No doubt Crazy Ma was changing the game. Taobao got a quick start with its free listings and continued to gain momentum as more and more users switched from eBay EachNet to Taobao. According to a Morgan Stanley report, Taobao was more customer focused and user friendly than eBay EachNet. With most users not sophisticated about auctions, the majority of Taobao's listings were for sales. Only 10 percent of its listings were for auctions, while eBay EachNet had about 40 percent of its listings for auctions. Taobao had also better terms for its customers: it offered longer listing periods (fourteen days) and let customers extend for one more period automatically. EBay EachNet did not have this flexibility.

Taobao's listings appeared to be more customer-centric while eBay EachNet's listings more product-centric. For example, Taobao's listings were organized into several categories, such as "Men," "Women," and so on, while eBay EachNet stuck to its global platform, grouping users into "Buyers" and "Sellers." At that time, China had about three hundred million cell phone users versus ninety million Internet users. Taobao offered instant messaging and voice mail to mobile phones for buyers and sellers because Chinese users were cell-phone savvy rather than computer savvy.[186]

It was clear that Taobao had an upper hand against its global counterpart because it really understood Chinese customers. As a result, Taobao had higher customer satisfaction than eBay EachNet. According to iResearch, a Beijing-based research firm, the user satisfaction level was 77 percent for Taobao versus 62 percent for eBay EachNet. The experience of competing with eBay gave Ma tremendous confidence. He was determined to win: "eBay may be a shark in the ocean, but I am a crocodile in the Yangtze River. If we fight in the ocean, we lose—but if we fight in the river, we win."[187]

In 2005, the battle between eBay and Taobao shifted to one of the key issues of e-commerce in China—the payment system. Most Chinese people did not have credit cards. Business transactions were either cash based or wired through banks. In the past, the payment and settlement risks were major obstacles that hindered e-commerce growth in China. EBay was lagging behind in offering its PayPal payment system because of the strict regulations for foreign banks. Knowing that the Chinese were accustomed to wiring money between their bank accounts, Ma introduced an online escrow payment system, AliPay, in January 2005. It allowed buyers to wire money from their bank accounts to Alibaba, which held the money in escrow until the products were satisfactorily delivered by sellers. AliPay killed two birds with one stone. It solved the settlement risk, ensuring that goods were delivered and payments were made between sellers and buyers. And, most incredibly, AliPay increased the liquidity in Taobao's marketplace, since it acted like a temporary bank between buyers and sellers.

AliPay was a key driver for Taobao's exponential growth. By March 2006, Taobao had outpaced eBay EachNet and became the leader in China's consumer-to-consumer (C2C) market, with 67 percent market share in terms of users, while eBay EachNet had only 29 percent market share.[188] "The competition is over," Ma exclaimed. "It's time to claim the battlefield."

On December 20, 2006, Meg Whitman flew to Shanghai to take part in a press conference to announce a new joint venture with Beijing-based Internet portal Tom Online, which provides wireless value-added multimedia services. It was, in reality, a formal announcement of eBay's withdrawal from the online auction market in China. EBay shut down its China site, eBay EachNet, and took a back seat to a tiny company with only $173 million in revenue and no experience in the online auction business.

"Open Sesame" for China's Alibaba

On November 4, 2007, Jack Ma's dream came true. The company he founded twelve years before, Alibaba.com, went public on the Hong Kong Stock Exchange and raised $1.5 billion, the second biggest IPO after Google. The *New York Times* labeled him "China's new Internet king,"[189] and many of his admirers referred to him as the "grandfather of the Internet in China."[190] In an interview with CNN, Ma said, "I never think about myself as an Internet king. I consider myself a teacher or CEO—chief education officer—of the China Internet market. I have studied the Internet in China since 1995. I set up the first Internet company in China, so today I can call myself China's chief education officer for the Internet."[191] This may be the secret of Ma's success.

By the end of 2007, Alibaba had twenty-five million registered users. In the world's most populous nation, where Internet users had already exceeded 160 million, Alibaba commanded a 69 percent market share in business-to-business (B2B) e-commerce.[192] If buyers entered the word "China" and "beer" into Alibaba's search engine, they found more than six thousand listings, including beer mugs, beer coolers, beer dispensers, etc. Its consumer e-commerce Web site, Taobao, had a market share of 83 percent, compared with 7 percent for eBay China.[193]

A self-portrayed "underdog" who could hardly get into college, Ma has been invited to speak at Harvard Business School and has delivered speeches at the World Economic Forum. As he reflected on his life, Ma said, "The most important thing is that we believed in our dream from day one. We made many mistakes, but we never gave up the hope of making sure our dream came true. One of the dreams that I wanted to realize when I set up my company in 1995, China Pages, was that if Jack Ma can be successful, then 80 percent of young people in and around the world can be successful!"[194]

The reason that mighty eBay lost its battle to a small guerilla company seems clear. Meg Whitman didn't ask her China team to look at the world upside down, as Jack Ma did.

First, eBay failed to recognize that the Chinese market and the business environment are very different from that of the West. EBay sent a German manager to lead the China operation and brought in a chief technology officer from the United States. Neither one spoke Chinese or understood the local market. It was eBay's biggest mistake. Second, because the top management team didn't understand the local market, they spent a lot of money doing the wrong things, such as advertising on the Internet in a country where small businesses didn't use the Internet. The fact that eBay had a strong brand in the United States didn't mean it would be a strong brand in China. Third, rather than adapt products and services to local customers, eBay stuck to its "global platform," which again did not fit local customers' tastes and preferences.

By ignoring differences between the East and West, eBay suffered a painful loss in one of the most important markets in the world.

Oneness in Competition: "If You Know Both Sides, You Know the Best Way"

In an interview with TalkAsia on CNN.com, Jack Ma said that because he understood English, he read a lot about the West and knew how poorly Western businesspeople understood China. That is the major reason some multinational corporations have failed miserably in China. One of the reasons Alibaba succeeded is because Jack Ma spent much more time studying American companies than any American company spent studying Chinese companies. As Jack Ma said, "If you know both sides, you know the best way."[195]

Like Jack Ma, the most successful competitors learn from their competition. They study and emulate their opponents' successful strategies. They analyze their opponents' strengths and weaknesses, and adapt their strategies and execution to exploit their own strengths and avoid their opponents' strengths. The most successful competitors also learn from their failures. They analyze them, find the flaw in execution, and adapt their behavior. Competition is a kind of forced learning—successes are rewarded and mistakes are weeded out, leading to ever-greater improvements and, ultimately, excellence. As the world becomes more interconnected, and as local companies like Alibaba become more world savvy, competition will increase. This is evident now in China, where numerous multinationals are entering China, seeking first to gain a foothold, and then to spread their presence throughout the vast country. But we also see Chinese companies making their competitive presences felt, now within China and soon outside of China. For example, Chinese car companies are expected to start exporting cars in significant numbers in the next few years. As the Japanese and Koreans before them, there is every reason to expect that they will succeed.

The global economy is becoming the playing field on which we all compete. As developing countries become more prosperous, their companies become more competitive, first in their own local markets, and eventually in the international arena. This is the expected flow of events. As globalization is helping to grow the Chinese middle class, the growing middle class is also creating correspondingly growing market opportunities in China for those companies able to compete there. Greater opportunities result in greater competition. Greater competition results in lower costs, greater efficiency, and higher quality products and services, all of which lead to an increase in the standard of living and to greater prosperity. These, in turn, lead to greater disposable income and a further expanding market, and the cycle continues.

Competition is therefore seen to be one of the engines for greater prosperity and opportunities. Although competition, when viewed through the lens of its local impact on an individual or a company, can be quite disruptive in the short term, from the larger view and in the longer term, healthy competition is beneficial. Viewed through this wider lens, competition serves to help raise standards of living around the world. In that way, oneness in competition implies that as other countries improve their competitiveness and seek their own niches in the global economy, their standard of living will rise while also creating new market opportunities for the rest of the world. Oneness in competition views global competition as intrinsic to the process of achieving prosperity for all.

Healthy competition creates incentives for improvement. Competition encourages us to know our strengths and to focus on them, to be the best that we can be. It also allows our competitors to find their own places in the competitive ecosystem. Oneness in competition views competition as inherent in the process of achieving excellence, that we better the world by being our best, and that we all ultimately benefit in a world where all are striving for improvement.

CHAPTER 8

Unquenchable Search for Meaning

"Happiness is the meaning and the purpose of life,
the whole aim and end of human existence"

– ARISTOTLE

ᗢ

On a beautiful spring day in 2008 in Shanghai, I met three young Chinese women for lunch: Veronica Chen, the head-hunter featured in chapter 2, Yolanda Wang, a public relations manager, and Rebecca Zhang, a saleswoman for a jewel company. Veronica, who had just turned thirty, was torn between two potential boyfriends. Yolanda, eldest of the three good friends, was living with a man who had just divorced. Rebecca, at twenty-nine the youngest of the three, did not have a suitor yet. To use her words, "I don't even have a candidate." At lunch, our conversation quickly turned to the biggest confusion in today's China: the role of religion and what people perceive as their purpose in life. An exploration of this topic can help us to understand the core values of the Chinese people as a nation. Here are some excerpts from their conversation:

"I have been on a spiritual quest, pursuing different religions," Yolanda said, looking pale. "I was very sick recently and thought I might die. But I said to myself: 'I cannot die because I haven't found a true religion yet.' "

"Yolanda has been searching from religion to religion," Veronica said, lighting a cigarette. The typical Chinese woman does not smoke cigarettes, but Veronica is not a typical Chinese woman. "I am interested in religion, but so far I cannot say which religion I believe in. I want to make sure. If I have one religion, I need to stick to it all my life."

"It's okay to change from religion to religion," Yolanda said. "If you don't get into it, you cannot fully understand it."

"I am like Veronica," said Rebecca. "I am interested in religion. I have friends who gave me the Bible, and I think many of the things they said make sense. But I don't feel like converting."

"Many people are searching," Veronica said. "But few can take that one step to convert."

"In our society, there are some moral codes and social norms that are considered good." Rebecca said. "Although I don't know how we got those codes and norms, I know somehow they are there. We have the basics of what is right and what is wrong. They are not from religion. I do not really feel I need a religion. Unless we come to a point that we cannot find answers from the social norms, then I may need to search for a religion."

"But our tradition—Buddhism and Confucianism—and value system were completely destroyed," Veronica said. "There is nothing for people to hang on to. Family relationships have changed dramatically, and the youth suicide rate is increasing. I am learning about psychotherapy—it came to China (from the West) recently and got a lot of attention (and support) from the government."

"I feel very few people are happy," Yolanda said. "If you ask me whether I am happy, I am not—because I don't know what I want the most."

"Aren't you happy with Philip?" Rebecca said. Philip is the man Yolanda was living with.

"But he is not what I want the most," Yolanda said.

"I am trying to have a good time, but I cannot say I am happy," Rebecca said, her eyes tearing up. "I don't even know what happiness is. It is something very elusive. If you ask me, here is what I think happiness means. I want to have a husband I love who loves me. I want us to live to be one hundred years old and still be together. I want to have three houses, one for us, one for my parents, and one for his parents, and we live close to each other. I also want you two good friends of mine living close to me. I do not want to have to worry about money. I want to have a chance to travel around the world. I hope for world peace—it will help me to travel. I hope I have many children. I hope all the people I care about are well."

"To me," Yolanda said, "if I don't have religion, my soul feels empty. It is horrible. But I have been to Christianity and other religions…now I am looking into Buddhism. If I can access Islam, I will investigate it, too. My central question is: why are we living—what's the meaning of life?"[196]

Religious Surge in China

What concerns these three young women has also concerned millions of Chinese people. China is undergoing rapid and profound changes. In the past three decades, the country has abandoned communist doctrine and focused entirely on commercial activities and economic development. Industrialization mixes in with the information revolution. Urbanization accompanies globalization. Amid these dramatic changes, social bonds broke down and traditional value systems fell apart. Conflicting moral values are competing with one another. In the past, communist belief served the function of religion. However, no one in China today believes in communism. A friend of mine said jokingly, "I don't even believe that Hu Jintao (president of China and general secretary of the Communist Party of China) believes in communism."

In a society that is becoming increasingly materialistic, many people are focusing on making money and getting rich. There has been serious moral decay in society. There is no trust in business dealings. Scandals about defective products that harmed or even caused the deaths of people or animals have repeatedly made headline news. In 2007, Mattel Inc., the world's largest toy maker, recalled 1.5 million Chinese-made toys that had excessive lead levels. After the scandal broke out, a Chinese toy factory owner, Zhang Shuhong, committed suicide. Before he died, he stated that his closest friend, who sold him the supposedly lead-free paint, cheated him.

Although middle class Chinese are economically better off, spiritually they feel deprived. When money cannot make them happy, they feel lost. They cannot find the center of their lives. "You saw many people become rich so quickly in a few years," Shi Jin-feng, a medical worker, said. "You would think they would be happy after they obtained all they wanted. But no—they are stressed and depressed. In the end, everything is a mirage. People found they are still not happy."[197]

On top of that, traditional family relationships are breaking apart. The divorce rate has increased dramatically. An increasing number of married men have mistresses. Infidelity has become a norm. Jenny Liu, a real estate broker in Wuhan, told me that, in Chinese tradition, the purpose of life was about family. Nevertheless, she was disillusioned about relationships and did not see herself getting married. Instead, she planned to adopt a child because that would give her a purpose in life.

Some people seek the pleasure of a good time, such as going to a bar, partying, or having sex. In the West, people know that China has become the world's largest market for many consumer products. Few realize that China is also becoming the world's largest semiporn entertainment center. People told me that China has the world's largest karaoke disco pubs with sauna escort girls. "I feel people's souls are really hungry," Shi Jin-feng said. "We have not been nurtured for so long—that's the source of all the suffering."

It is not surprising that many people turn to religion for answers. There is a surge in religious belief to fill the void. A 2006 survey by the Pew Global Attitudes Project says, "Thirty-one percent of the Chinese public considers religion to be very or somewhat important in their lives, compared with only 11 percent who say religion is not at all important." [198] A study by researchers at Shanghai's East China Normal University found that "31.4 percent of Chinese aged sixteen and above, or about three hundred million, are religious."[199]

Religions in China

China has four main recognized religions: Buddhism, Christianity, Islam, and Taoism. Buddhists represent the largest religious group in China, making up about 15 percent of the adult population.[200] Tibetan Buddhism has become more popular in Chinese cities in recent years. Many urbanites are attracted to it because they consider it spiritually more pure and without rigid rituals.[201] The state news agency Xinhua identifies the total number of Chinese Buddhists at "approximately one hundred million."

Christianity is China's second-largest officially recognized religion, and Chinese government figures indicate dramatic growth in both Protestants and Catholics. The government banned Bibles until the late 1970s. Now, the country's largest Bible factory prints more than six million religious books a year. The officially reported number of Christians increased 50 percent in less than ten years.[202] In reality, the number may be much larger. The largest and fastest-growing group of Christians is people belonging to independent Christian churches, widely known as "house churches." The World Christian Database estimates that there are approximately seventy million Chinese associated with more than three hundred house church networks. Zhao Xiao, a former Communist Party official and convert to Christianity, said that there are up to 130 million Christians in China.[203]

Islam came to China in the seventh century when Persian and Central Asian merchants travelled to China for trade. The exact number of Muslims is difficult to determine. According to government figures, there are about twenty million Muslims in China today. Many of them are in Xinjiang province, where ethnic conflicts have increased in recent years. Some are in the Ningxia Hui autonomous region in midwest China. Today, some mosques date back to as early as the Tang Dynasty (618-907).

Taoism is based on the *Dao De Jing,* written by Lao Zi (sixth century BC). The central concept of Taoism is *the Way*, which regulates natural processes in the universe and embodies the harmony of opposites (i.e., there would be no love without hate, no light without darkness, no male without female.). In Taoism, everything in the universe is constantly changing. A particular state reaches equilibrium or stability when yin and yang—two primal opposite forces in the universe—are harmoniously balanced. Taoist beliefs have shaped Chinese thought for ages, more than any other religion or philosophy. Based on Taoist beliefs, the Chinese tend to see the seemingly chaotic world to be operating with an unseen order—the Way. They believe that changes are inevitable; events evolve as a process; and opposite forces in the universe, such as yin and yang, balance dynamically. This kind of thinking, although not taught in formal education in modern times, has been passed down from generation to generation. It is as embedded in their souls as a fish naturally swimming in the river, and even the most uneducated peasants think this way.

In everyday life, Taoism has become a popular folk religion with a range of gods and spirits, such as gods of fortune and health. The Pew poll found that three out of five Chinese express a personal belief in supernatural phenomena. The Chinese are practical people, and so religion has become a practical matter.

Rural people often worship the god of earth or the god of water to ensure a good harvest. Business people consult the god of fortune before they make an important business decision. Ordinary people bestow food and fruit at the temples to appeal to the god of health.

The Government's Attitude toward Religion

Religion in China is a complicated matter. Before the reform, religion was discouraged, as it fundamentally contradicted communist atheist ideology. After the reform, the situation gradually changed. Now, the Chinese government has realized that religion has an important function in society, and it commends religions that promote social stability.

In 2005, international research firm InterMedia conducted a survey of more than ten thousand people across twenty-one provinces and found that 33 percent of Communist Party officials and government employees are very or somewhat interested in religion.[204] In recent years, many members of the Communist Party have become Buddhists.

However, because of concern for maintaining stability and national sovereignty, the Chinese government does not allow allegiance to a foreign authority, such as the pope. Therefore, Chinese Catholics worship through the Chinese Catholic Patriotic Association rather than the Roman Catholic Church. The government is also against cults, which it considers deceptive and harmful.

Nevertheless, religion is now encouraged as a positive force in Chinese society. In April 2006, China hosted the first Buddhist conference in Hangzhou and invited Buddhist leaders from around the world (except the Dalai Lama). The official media gave the conference considerable coverage. The theme of the conference was "A Harmonious World Begins in the Mind," which echoed President Hu Jintao's call to build a "harmonious society." For the Chinese people, who have long been weary from Mao's class struggle as well as chaotic changes in recent years, the concept of harmony resonates with them well.

The Search for Spirituality

Dong Lu, an entrepreneur who has an Internet start-up called Beyond Tailor, recently converted to Christianity. It was not an easy step for him because the concept of a personified deity like Jesus Christ is foreign to him, as is the concept of the original Creation. Growing up in an atheist family in Beijing, religion played no role in his life. "I believe in science," Dong used to say. "I believe in evolution." I understand exactly how Dong Lu felt. I remember that when I grew up, religion was the equivalent of superstition. It was associated with ignorance and backwardness. Like Dong Lu, I was raised to believe in science, not superstition.

Although not religious, Dong was raised with strong ethics. His family members are all intellectuals—professors and scholars. Dong Lu, however, did not follow the family tradition of attending college. He went to a vocational school to study fashion design. It was not a conventional major, and his parents strongly opposed it. Nevertheless, Dong defied his parents' wishes. Still, Dong was disappointed with the school and dropped out two years later. He went on to become an entrepreneur, selling computer software and magazines. Although he made a handsome profit, Dong felt that he was not respected in a society where only educated people enjoyed the highest prestige.

"Everyone in my family has a university degree," Dong said. "I was like a black sheep." Dong decided to go to Japan to continue his college education. In Japan, he washed dishes in restaurants while working on his degree. Against all odds, he finished college in Japan and got a job at Goldman Sachs.

"On my first day," Dong said, "my boss asked me: 'do you want to make one million dollars or do you want to make one billion dollars?' I thought both numbers sounded astronomical to me and there was no difference. So I said, 'I want to make one million dollars.' Then my boss said I was the right person for the job. I was at Goldman for two years and got to know many rich people in Japan. But I was not happy. My job was to make rich people even richer. One day, while trying to close a deal before midnight, I watched CNN and saw a story about Grameen Bank. I was deeply touched when I saw a woman use a microloan to make baskets and sell them at the market. Her life changed, all because she got a loan of $50. And I was making a $5 million trade for a client. When I made a phone call to him for his approval of the trade, I overheard karaoke music and a woman's sexy voice saying, 'This ice cream is mine...' At that moment, I realized that I was so disconnected from reality. I did not know what value I had created. I felt my life had no meaning."

Dong Lu decided to leave his job. He applied to Stanford Graduate School of Business, and it admitted him. "Stanford really helped to shape my view of life," Dong said. "Now, I am very confident in myself. I know I can achieve anything if I put my mind to it. I want to make a difference." That was a Stanford mantra—"to make a difference"—which I am quite familiar with.

After business school, Dong went back to China and started an Internet company. A friend invited him to attend Bible study in his church. At first, Dong resisted, but eventually went. "I have always admired people who have strong faith," Dong said. "I have secretly believed that there might be something that is beyond everything—that people call 'God.' " His epiphany came when he realized God is not an old man with a white beard in the sky. "God is in my heart," he said, "and Christianity is about love." Although Dong was not fully convinced, he was willing to walk down the path and give religion a try. "There is no harm," he said. "And I have one more choice (to believe in God)."

Dong Lu saw that there were many problems in China because people did not fear God. "People could do anything without fearing the consequences," Dong said. "China is not just a big country;

China is a big country without faith. If a country has many rich people who have no faith, it is worse than a country that is poor and faithless. If you do not have money, you cannot do too much harm. But if you have money, but no conscience, it is worse. For example, if I am a successful businessman and I do not have a mistress, I am considered abnormal. China has become a society of deformity—*heibai diandao* (black and white reversed)."[205]

I have met quite a few people who are as critical and outspoken as Dong Lu. I believe China has a "faith crisis." However, I also think China is in the process of readjusting. As traditional values are reviving, more people are becoming spiritual.

Karen Liu, a returnee who became an entrepreneur and angel investor, flew around the country to attend Buddhist retreats. Li Miaoyu, a laid-off worker who became an *Ayi*, a maid who does household chores for several families, told me that her church grew from fewer than fifty members in 2005 to more than five thousand members two years later. One young woman, who worked in the IBM China procurement department, applied to Stanford Graduate School of Business. The application form asked her to write an essay about what kind of person she wanted to become. It was a simple question, but she had never thought about it. The more she considered the question, the more she felt she could not answer it. It became a problem for her. She started to read the Bible, Koran, and other holy writings. Whether she found her answer I am not sure, but she told a friend, "I have never felt so close to God."[206]

In recent years, there has also been a revival of Confucianism. Many Confucius institutes have been established around the country. A friend of mine, Hong Ping, started a Confucius institute in Zhuhai that has received a lot of favorable publicity from the media and support from the government.

Dong Lu felt more grounded after he became a Christian. He believed he gained inner strength and could face many temptations. "I used to have a lot of ego and vanity, but now I have a purpose in life." Dong Lu was spending a lot of time performing community service. He loved to help seniors. Every week, he went to a senior home to help a wheelchaired old woman, carrying her into and out of the hospital.

My Spiritual Journey

It takes a lot of soul searching to figure out one's purpose in life. Since I came to America, I have gone through an intense spiritual search. My experience was very similar to Yolanda's and Dong Lu's experiences. Coming from a country where people worshiped Mao like a god, I could not be more cynical about any religion that could control my mind. On the other hand, I was earnestly searching for a purpose in my life. I was confused and lost, and felt that any material "success" that I attained could not quench the thirst inside me. I explored just about everything, from Christianity to the Baha'i faith to Taoism, in a quest to find that eternal, incorruptible truth that some call God.

My understanding of spirituality came with a fundamental shift in the worldview on which I was raised. Although the world is physical, made of materials such as atoms and particles, I came to see that human beings are essentially spiritual beings, which separates us from animals. While animals act on instinct, humans can rise above instinct and choose to be noble because we have a soul, the essence of the Infinite that is beyond our finite mind. To me, all the religions in the world are like one divine book sent down by one God. Each religion is like one chapter of the same book; each chapter teaches the same principles such as love, unity, and peace. The differences among religions derive more from differences in cultures and traditions, so that people may find it easier to integrate religious practices into their daily lives.

My limited understanding of spirituality would soon be tested when I faced a life-and-death situation. In the winter of 2000-2001, I returned to China to see my uncle, who was suffering from lung cancer that was already in its final stages. Doctors gave him only about six to nine months to live. When I arrived at the hospital, his daughter told me that the end was near and he had not been able to speak a word for days. As I walked into the room, holding a bouquet of flowers in my hand, I was saddened, feeling guilty that I may have come too late.

My uncle's face lit up when he saw me. Then he did something that surprised everyone in the room. "This…is my-y niece… Haiyan!" he managed to stutter these words with much difficulty. I could not say a word, trying to swallow my tears. He looked tired and frail. His hands were not as strong as before. However, beneath his failing body, I still saw his strong spirit—the cheerful, warm, and forever optimistic person he had always been.

My uncle is the most honorable man I have ever known. He was the person I admired most when growing up. He is still the person I admire most in the world. Although I did not see him often as we lived in different cities, my uncle had inspired and influenced me profoundly both as a child and as an adult. Even today, I can still recite the little poem he wrote for me when I entered elementary school and got my first A grades: "Haiyan is a good girl, getting awards at school. Study hard and move up, making progress every day."[207]

Later, after I came to the United States, whenever I talked to him on the phone, he was always encouraging and inspiring. He would say something like, "I hope you will fly even higher" (a reference to my name, which means "sea swallow"). He was full of wisdom and kindness, always thought about others, and never complained about any problem or hardship in his own life.

My uncle was born into an intellectual family in Shandong province. His grandfather was a member of Dr. Sun Yet-sen's Revolutionary Alliance and participated in the overthrow of the Qing dynasty. As a teenager, my uncle attended a Christian high school started by missionaries from the United States. In the 1930s, China underwent a series of calamities. Years of civil war and social disruption bankrupted the economy. In 1937, the Japanese invaded China, burning villages, killing people, and raping women. My uncle was only thirteen years old at that time. He was deeply concerned about China's misfortune and wanted to do something to help his country.

Under the influence of his teacher, who was an underground communist, my uncle was attracted to communist ideals. "Working men of all countries, unite!" Marx's *Communist Manifesto* states. "The proletarians have nothing to lose but their chains. They have a world to win."[208] At age fifteen, he joined the Communist Party to fight against the Japanese invasion. He vowed that he would not return home until all the "Japanese devils" were driven out of China.

After 1949, my uncle rose to become one of the youngest leaders in the Communist Party and held important positions in the central government. He worked tirelessly to rebuild a new China. At the beginning of the Cultural Revolution, my uncle was among the first to see problems. He rallied a few brave colleagues to write a letter to Chairman Mao, reporting chaotic fights among the masses and the Red Guards. For that, my uncle was accused of "oppressing the students' movement," and labeled as the biggest *zouzipai*, or "capitalist." Today, China has been taken over by a capitalist mania. In those days, however, the worst thing you could do was to call someone a "capitalist." Consequently, my uncle was denounced by the Red Guards, and later was quarantined in a cowshed and severely persecuted.

After Deng Xiao Ping returned to power in 1976, my uncle had new hope and resumed his work. He was at one time the vice president of Peking University, the equivalent of Harvard in China. Students loved him and respected him. People who worked with him were all impressed by his integrity and principles. During the 1989 Tiananmen Square students' demonstration, my uncle stood up against all the pressure from the hardliners within the Party in order to protect the students. He was then removed from his post and purged from the Party as punishment.

My uncle never told me any of this. I learned later from an outpouring of memorial articles from his former colleagues and students. However, I did know one thing: my uncle was bewildered and heartbroken in his later years. Were all the ideals that he held so dear not real? Was the cause that he had devoted his entire life to a mistake? Was his life's work in vain? To an atheist as my uncle was, the end of one's life is the end of everything. At his deathbed, I thought to myself, "What could I do to comfort him, to cheer him as he used to cheer me? What could I say to him that his life would not be in vain, and that his dreams for a better world would live on?" In a parable to show him that there is a God, and that our lives do not end in this world, I started to tell him a story:

"Before a butterfly became a butterfly, it was a worm inside a cocoon. The worm thought the cocoon was everything in its world, until one day it broke the cocoon to become a beautiful butterfly. Then it realized there was another, far superior realm that it was not able to comprehend when it was a worm inside a cocoon. The end of the life of the worm was the beginning of the life of the butterfly."

My uncle looked at me with his tender gaze, and I instantly knew that he understood what I was trying to tell him. That night, he passed away in peace.

If before I had doubted that God existed, at that moment I was beyond any doubt. I truly believe that my uncle has passed on to the next world, where all the mysteries in this life would be made plain, all questions would be answered, and all the sacrifices my uncle had endured would prove to be worthwhile. His spirit lives on.

My uncle was a true idealist, a true patriot, a person with great integrity who loved his country, his family, and everyone he came across. He had touched so many lives. At his funeral, people came from near and far to pay final tribute to him. In their eulogies, they remembered him for the spiritual essence of who he was: "an honorable person," "a visionary and courageous leader," "an optimist," "an inspiring mentor," "a compassionate colleague," and "a loving father and uncle." My uncle will always be an inspiration that reminds me what kind of person I want to become.

My uncle may have been disillusioned with the Communist Party, but he never gave up on his noble ideals throughout his life. At the funeral, it occurred to me that Marx's writing inspired my uncle in the same way that Abraham Lincoln's and Martin Luther King's writings inspired me. Communism as an economic system has clearly failed. Communism as a political system has produced brutal dictatorships. Yet, to think that people inside the Communist Party are all "goons and thugs" is wrong. I know for a fact there are other people like my uncle inside the Communist Party in China who are trying to do the best for the country. I have no illusions that hardliners exist in China who hold extreme views, as they do in the United States. Some people still view China through the lens of a Cold War mentality. The Cold War was a very unfortunate episode in recent human history. However, it ended twenty years ago. It is time to move on.

"To Love All Humankind"

The world *has* moved on. However, in order for us truly to move on, we need to adopt a new way—a spiritual way—to look at the world. The following story has inspired me, and I hope it will inspire you as well.

Yan Yan, chief financial officer of SOHO China, a Beijing property developer, flew to seven countries in nine days. She worked countless hours and met with hundreds of investors in preparation for the company's initial public offering (IPO). SOHO China, an acronym for "small office, home office," was founded in 1995 by a flamboyant couple, Zhang Xin and Pan Shiyi. In twelve years, Yan Yan worked her way up from an assistant to become an executive manager. Most of the company's projects are residential and commercial developments, targeting the expanding middle class.

One of the company's crown jewels, Jianwai SOHO in Beijing's central business district, consists of eighteen residential towers, two office towers, and four villas in downtown Beijing that boast light, airy apartments, trendy restaurants, and art galleries.

When the company went public on the Hong Kong Stock Exchange in 2007, it raised nearly $1.7 billion. Although excited as well as exhausted, Yan Yan maintained a Zenlike composure with gentle eye contact and a warm smile. Her financial success was certainly something to cherish. Yet, that was not her ultimate purpose in life. According to Yan Yan, she found her center and gained her strength from her faith.

Two years before, Yan Yan was on the verge of a breakdown. In addition to the stress from work, Yan Yan could not make sense of what she was doing every day at work. People she interacted with—developers and investors—seemed to care only about making money. Every day, she saw only greed. There was no trust among people and no integrity in business dealings. She was depressed. She found herself wandering the Buddhist temples in the mountains, hoping to escape life.

By happenstance, she attended a training class in her company called "New Thinking Creates a New Reality." The idea that "humanity is like flowers in a garden" attracted her. Though differing in kind, color, form, and shape, they are nourished by the rays of one sun and refreshed by the waters of one spring. The diversity of different colors and shapes increases their charm and adds to their beauty. She realized how boring it would be if all the flowers and plants, the leaves and blossoms, were all the same shape and color. It was an epiphany for Yan Yan that love is the one thing that changes everything in life. She said, "The world would be a much better place if each and every one of us can have love not just for our own families but also for all humanity."

Later, Yan Yan learned that these concepts are from the Baha'i faith, a religion she had never heard of. The Baha'i faith is a monotheistic religion founded by Baha'u'llah in Persia in

1844, emphasizing the spiritual unity of all humankind. Baha'is view the world's major religions as progressive revelations from God through divine messengers that include Abraham, Moses, Buddha, Zoroaster, Jesus Christ, and Muhammad. The central theme of Baha'u'llah's message is that humanity is one single race and that the day has come for humanity's unification into one global society.

Now Yan Yan felt more centered. Every now and then, she would bring her son to visit orphanages in Beijing. Mother Teresa was her heroine. Whenever she held those homeless children who were severely disabled, she felt tremendous love that she had never felt before. The satisfaction she felt to love someone she did not know was beyond words and far greater than any material gains. Yan Yan spent a lot of her leisure time in charity work. Much of it was devoted to education. "It is not just education for knowledge," she said. "But also spiritual education: to love oneself, love others and love all humankind."[209]

Oneness in Spirit: "Out of Many, We are One"

The middle classes in China and the West have many common values. Whether we are Chinese, American, European, Asian, or African, we are all human beings. Essentially, we are all longing for the same things, such as true fulfillment. At some point in our lives, we all ask the same questions, as Yolanda did: Why are we living? What is the purpose of life?

We also realize that both middle class Chinese and Westerners are struggling to balance material gains and spiritual enlightenment. Material advancement alone cannot ensure happiness. As we have seen in China, people are economically better off, but spiritually impoverished. They frequently encounter greed and moral decay. The same problems exist in America as well as the rest of the world. The single-minded quest for money is at the root of many problems in the United States. Recently, it caused the Wall Street meltdown that affected millions of people. On the other hand, spirituality alone does not have much meaning in the modern world. When taken to extremes, it can be very dangerous, as we have seen terrorists killing many innocent people in the name of "God."

Material civilization and spiritual civilization are like the *yin and yang* of the universe. It is essential to balance the two. Just as an overemphasis on religious doctrine leads to fundamentalism, excessive pursuit of material gain leads to materialism. We can see material civilization as a lamp and spiritual civilization as the light. The lamp without light is dark, and light needs the lamp to shine. Material advancement and spiritual enrichment must go hand in hand like two wings of a bird. Only when material and spiritual civilizations are linked and balanced, like *yin and yang*, will humanity achieve true fulfillment.

If we can see that we are all beings of one God, and our souls reflect the essence of one God, surely all the people in the world are one, from the same one Source. As Yan Yan observed, humanity is like the flowers in a garden. Although they differ in kind, color, form, and shape, they are nourished by the rays of one sun and refreshed by the waters of one spring. Unity in diversity is achieved as different colors and shapes add beauty to the entire garden.

EPILOGUE

From the Chinese
Dream to One World One Dream

"The earth is but one country and mankind its citizens."

- BAHA'U'LLAH

ᕫᕽ

The Twenty-ninth Olympic Games have come and gone. The world is far from "One World, One Dream." Terrorist threats, trade wars, ideological conflicts, climate changes, and natural disasters occupy the headlines. Although "One World, One Dream" is not what the world is today, it is what the world should be, and we should not settle for the distance between the two.

Oneness is not a false hope or wishful thinking. It reflects an eternal physical and spiritual reality that we are interconnected and interdependent. Science supports the reality of oneness. Anthropology, physiology, psychology, sociology, and, especially, genetics in the decoding of the human genome show that all humans are similar, although we are quite diverse in the details of our personalities and lives. The world's great religions also support the spiritual principle of oneness, as their founders have all preached the common spiritual unity of humanity.

From *The Chinese Dream*, we can see that middle class Chinese and Westerners are connected by a common set of core values. We belong to the same world, and we share the same aspirations and dreams. We desire an education for our children. We are concerned about providing for our retirement and for our families' health care. We are interested in leaving something behind for the next generation. We are concerned for global stability.

We also have notable differences, but our differences are complementary rather than contradictory. Our differences are not either-or choices. By combining them, we get the best of both worlds. When we see these differences as the strengths that they truly are, by exploiting our interdependence and learning from each other, we can leverage both sides of the same coin, and we all benefit. We will become stronger as we embrace unity in diversity.

Humanity is collectively coming of age as globalization and technology now allow everyone in the world to connect, interact, perceive our interdependence, and become conscious of our oneness. The trend towards globalization is evident in the growth in the numbers and scope of international organizations of all kinds, from inter-governmental organizations, to international non-governmental organizations (NGOs) and multinational corporations. The growth of these organizations demonstrates the growing need for people to work together across national boundaries. Technology, in particular telecommunications technology and the Internet, has further enabled this international cooperation by facilitating the sharing of information and knowledge.

Examples of our interdependence abound. Economically, the prosperity of each individual depends inherently on the interconnections of trade; otherwise, we would all have to grow our own food and build our own houses. In our modern, highly interwoven world, economic prosperity depends heavily on *global* trade. Environmentally, we suffer if our neighbor pollutes our air or water, whether our neighbor is conscious or not of the damage done. With our large-scale environmental challenges, polluters on the other side of the globe are really our neighbors, since they can cause acid rain or atmospheric warming that can impact us directly. We are all in the same boat—this ark we call Earth. We have *always* been interdependent in this way, but in the past we were simply less aware of our environmental impact on others. Politically, our interdependence is very evident in our need to work out agreeable political solutions to our mutual problems, whether in regard to trade, the environment, security, responding to natural disasters, or other global issues. Our ability to live peacefully and harmoniously as global neighbors depends on our recognition of our interdependence.

The oneness of the world is not only what the world needs today, it is what the world is asking for. Millions of people and countless organizations have already taken steps to address the serious challenges facing humanity in the twenty-first century. For example, Web sites like worldchanging.com and treehugger.com provide information on sustainable technologies and practices that highlight our interdependence and seek to share ideas and solutions to our global environmental challenges. The dream of a world of peace and unity, and a world that works for all people on the planet, has continued to inspire people around the world.

The Chinese middle class, as the focus of this book, is an emerging global force that is a catalyst for us to realize our global oneness. I encourage you to take actions in your own community, whether it is your work, your church, or your school, to bring greater awareness of the interconnectedness and interdependence of the world, and to embrace the benefits of this oneness. The prosperity of humankind can only be achieved when different nations interact harmoniously as if part of one human body.

NOTES

1. McKinsey Global Institute, "From 'Made in China' to 'Sold in China': The Rise of the Chinese Urban Consumer," 2006.

2. Zheng He (1371-1435), an ancient Chinese explorer and mariner who made voyages to Southeast Asia, South Asia, and East Africa.

3. The Emperor Qianlong (1711-1799) was the fifth emperor of the Manchu-led Qing Dynasty.

4. The Treaty of Nanking, the first of what the Chinese consider were unequal treaties between China and the United Kingdom, was signed in 1842. China paid the British an indemnity, ceded the territory of Hong Kong, and agreed to establish a "fair and reasonable" tariff.

5. The Cultural Revolution was a period of widespread social and political upheaval in China between 1966 and 1976, resulting in nationwide chaos and economic disarray.

6. Pew Research Center, "View of China's Economic and Military Power," Pew Global Attitudes Projects, June 17, 2010, http://pewglobal. org/2010/06/17/obama-more-popular-abroad-than-at-home/6/#chapter-5-views-of-china (accessed July 21, 2010).

7. Credit Suisse, "Credit Suisse survey shows Chinese consumer spending jumps," Jan. 12, 2011, (https://www.credit-suisse.com/news/en/media release.jsp?ns=41389).

8. Jonathan Woetzel, Janamitra Devan, et al., "Preparing for China's Urban Billion," McKinsey Global Institute, March 2008.

9. Clay Chandler, "China's Mobile Maestro," *Fortune*, July 31, 2007.

10. Barry Wilkinson, Markus Eberhardt, and Andrew Millington, "On the Performance of Chinese State-owned and Private Enterprises: The View from Foreign-invested Enterprises," *Journal of General Management*, Vol. 32, No. 1 (Autumn 2006).

11. The Qiantang River, also known as the Qian River, is located in southeast China. The river originates in the borders of Anhui and Jiangxi provinces and passes through Hangzhou before flowing into the East China.

12. Abraham Lincoln, Gettysburg Address, November 19, 1863.

13. Sonia M. L. Wong, "China's Stock Market: A Marriage of Capitalism and Socialism," *Cato Journal* 26, no. 3 (Fall 2006), p. 389.

14. Peter S. Goodman, "China to Allow More Stock Sales," *Washington Post*, August 25, 2006, http://www.washingtonpost.com/wp-dyn/content/article/2005/08/24/AR2005082402246.html (accessed December 6, 2007).

15. Guy S. Liu, Pei Sun, and Wing Thye Woo, "The Political Economy of Chinese-Style Privatization: Motives and Constraints," *World Development* 34, no. 12 (December 2006): pp. 2016-2033.

16. "The Second Long March," *Economist*, December 19, 2008, p. 30.

17. Chen Ling, interview by author, Hangzhou, China, September 7, 2007, followed up with e-mails.

18. Lian Fang, Lian Su's brother, interview by author, Hangzhou, China, September 10, 2007.

19. Huang Yong, interview by author, September 16, 2007.

20. Liu Jie and Tong Hao, "Private Companies Playing a Bigger Role," *China Daily*, Jan. 29, 2008, http://www.chinadaily.com.cn/bizchina/2008-01/29/content_6428007.htm (accessed November 21, 2008).

21. "More College Students Joining the Communist Party," Xinhua News Agency, October 29, 2003, http://www.china.org.cn/english/government/78652.htm (accessed June 30, 2010).

22. Wu Haitao, interview by author, Hangzhou, China, August 10, 2007.

23. The poem was translated by the author.

24. Paul Gao, "Selling China's Cars to the World: An Interview with Chery's CEO," *McKinsey Quarterly*, May 2008.

25. The Economist, " The Rise of State Capitalism," January 21, 2012.

26. Tini Tran, "Chinese Officials Fled Overseas with $50 Billion," Associated Press, January 11, 2010.

27. "China Food Safety Head Executed," BBC News, July 10, 2007.

28. A Chinese idiom.

29. Chen Ling, interview by author, September 7, 2007.

30. Veronica Chen, interview by author, Shanghai, China, August 27, 2007.

31. Ying Hui-er, interview by author, Shanghai, China, June 6, 2008.

32. "Understanding China's 'Angry Youth': What does the Future Hold?" Brookings Institution, Washington, D. C., April 29, 2009.

33. Curtis Chin, interview by author, Guangzhou, China, May 7, 2008.

34. Andrew Kohut and Richard Wike, "China's Optimism: Prosperity Brings Satisfaction–and Hope," 2005 Pew Global Attitudes Survey, The Pew Global Attitudes Project, November 16, 2005.

35. Liu Xueshan, interview by author, Chongqing, China, May 15, 2008.

36. "The Foxconn Suicides," *Wall Street Journal*, May 27, 2010, http://online. wsj.com/article/SB1000142405274870426920457527003132323762 38.html (accessed July 6, 2010).

37. Michael Wines, "Attacker Stabs 28 Chinese Children," *New York Times*, April 29, 2010.

38. "China's healthcare reform one year later: What's changed?" InMedica Research, March 16, 2010.

39. "China unveils health-care reform guidelines," Xinhua News Agency, April 6, 2009.

40. Gordon Fairclough, "Beijing Plans $124 Billion Overhaul of Health Care," *Wall Street Journal*, January 22, 2009, page A8.

41. Victor Ku, interview by author, Guangzhou, China, May 10, 2008.

42. "China's Healthcare Reform: One Year On," InMedica, March 22, 2010.

43. Eddie Liu, interview by author, Shanghai, China, August 27, 2007.

44. Wu Xiaoguang and Zhang Huimei, interview by author, Yangtze River, China, May 19, 2008.

45. The Economist, "A Nation of City Slickers," Jan. 21, 2012

46. Jonathan Woetzel, Janamitra Devan, Luke Jordan, Stefano Negri, and Dian Farrell, "Preparing for China's Urban Billion," McKinsey Global Institute, March 2008.

47. Janamitra Devan, Stefane Negri, and Johathan R. Woetzel, "Meeting the Challenges of China's Growing Cities," *McKinsey Quarterly*, July 2008. The 2010 figure is derived according to "China Urbanization Interactive Map," McKinsey Global Institute, http://www.mckinsey.com/mgi/publications/china_Urban_Billion/slideshow/main.asp (accessed July 2, 2010).

48. Janamitra Devan, Stefance Gegri, and Jonathan R. Woetzel, "Meeting the Challenges of China's Growing Cities," *McKinsey Quarterly*, July 2008.

49. Zhang Ye, "Hope for China's Migrant Women Workers," *China Business Review*, 2002.

50. Yi Fan, interview by author, Hangzhou, China, September 5, 2007, followed up November 4, 2007.

51. Bahá'u'lláh, *Gleanings,* 1848, p. 250.

52. Michael Wines, "Local Court Is China's First to Accept a Tainted-Milk Suit," *New York Times*, March 26, 2009.

53. Yi Fan, interview by author, Hangzhou, China, September 5, 2007, followed up November 4, 2007.

54. Hu Shanhua, interview by author, Beijing, China, August 18, 2007.

55. "China Has 25 Million College Students," Xinhua News Agency, October 18, 2007.

56. Lian Fang, interview by author, September 10, 2007.

57. Guo Jiaxue, "Academic Corruption Undermining Higher Education: Yau Shing-tung," *China Daily*, June 2, 2010.

58. Willy Lam, "Perpetual Challenges to China's Education Reform," *China Brief* 6, no. 24 (May 9, 2007).

59. Mary Hennock, "To Save the Chinese Dream," *Newsweek*, February 7, 2009.

60. Schmittzehe & Partners, "Made in China: Moving Up the Value Chain," 2009.

61. Technician Number 30, interview by author, Beijing, China, August 9, 2007.

62. Figure from IHS Global Insight, quoted by Peter Marsh, "U.S. Manufacturing Crown Slips," *Financial Times*, June 20, 2009.

63. According to a study by the Institute for International Economics, by C. Fred Bergsten, Bates Gill, Nicholas R. Lardy, and Derk Mitchell, in *China: The Balance Sheet, What the World Needs to Know Now About the Emerging Superpower* (New York, Public Affairs, 2006), chapter 1, p. 10.

64. "The People's Republic of Capitalism," Discovery Channel, July 2008.

65. "In China, To Get Rich is Glorious," *Businessweek*, February 6, 2006, http://www.businessweek.com/magazine/content/06_06/b3970072.htm (accessed November 19, 2009)

66. "China's Rich Have $1.1 Trillion Hidden Income, Study Finds" *Bloomberg News*, August 12, 2010, http://www.bloomberg.com/news/2010-08-12/china-s-wealthy-have-as-much-as-1-1-trillion-in-hidden-income-study-says.html (accessed August 18, 2010).

67. "Meet Chinese Consumers of 2020," McKinsey Quarterly, March 2012.

68. Zhou Jie, interview by author, Beijing, China, August 9, 2007.

69. Wikipedia, "Xujiahui," http://en.wikipedia.org/wiki/Xujiahui, (accessed March 12, 2009).

70. "China 2010 Auto Sales Reach 18 Million," Bloomberg, January 10, 2011, http://www.bloomberg.com/news/2011-01-10/china-2010-auto-sales-reach-18-million-extend-lead-update1-.html (accessed Apr. 2, 2012).

71. David Barboza, "China, New Land of Shoppers, Builds Malls on Gigantic Scale," *New York Times*, May 25, 2005, http://www.nytimes.com/2005/05/25/business/worldbusiness/25mall.html (accessed February 23, 2009).

72. Zhu Yiping, interview by author, Shanghai, China, June 5, 2008.

73. HSBC, quoted in Peter Wong, "Raiding the Piggy Bank", *Time*, February 22, 2007, http://www.time.com/time/magazine/article/0,9171,1592583,00.html.

74. "Burgeoning Bourgeoisie: A Special Report on the New Middle Classes," *Economist*, February 14, 2009, p. 3.

75. "The Great Leap Online," *The Economist*, Nov. 26, 2011, http://www.economist.com/node/21540260 (accessed Apr. 2, 2012). Shaun Rein, "In China, Online Shopping Soars," Forbes.com, June 25, 2008, http://www.forbes.com/home/2008/06/24/internet-retail-sales-oped-cx_sr_0625china.html (accessed June 26, 2008).

76. China Statistical Yearbook, 2006 data, published in "Why do Chinese Households Save So Much?" International Economic Trends, August 2008, Federal Reserve Bank of St. Louis. Another commonly quoted saving rate is the total saving rate, which includes the public sector. The total

saving rate is even higher, in the neighborhood of 50% or more. "China's Stimulus Package: Will It Work, and What's Next?" Knowledge@ Wharton, November 19, 2008, http://www.knowledgeatwharton.com. cn/index.cfm?fa=viewfeature&languageid=1&articleid=1954 (accessed December 10, 2008).

77. Diana Farrell, Eric Beinhocker, Ulrich Gersch, Ezra Greenberg, Elizabeth Stephenson, Jonathan Ablett, Mingyu Guan, and Janamitra Devan, "From 'Made in China' to 'Sold in China': The rise of the Chinese urban consumer," McKinsey Global Institute, December 2006, p. 63.

78. "Unlocking the Power of Chinese Consumers: An Interview with Stephen Roach," *McKinsey Quarterly*, August 2009, https://www.mckinseyquar- terly.com/ghost.aspx?ID=/Unlocking_the_power_of_Chinese_consum- ers_An_interview_with_Stephen_Roach_2428.

79. China Market Research Group (CMR) survey of five hundred young adults, cited by Shaun Rein in "China's Rising Retail Market," *Businessweek*, April 2, 2008, http://www.businessweek.com/globalbiz/ content/apr2008/gb2008042_054897.htm (accessed December 10, 2008). "How Half the World Shops: Apparel in Brazil, China, and India," *McKinsey Quarterly*, November 4, 2007.

80. Andrew Jacobs, "China's Economy, in Need of Jump Start, Waits for Citizens' Fists to Loosen," *International Herald Tribune*, December 3, 2008, http://www.iht.com/articles/2008/12/03/asia/03china.php (accessed December 10, 2008).

81. "IKEA Maintains China Expansion Plans," China Retail News, September 17, 2007, http://www.chinaretailnews.com/2007/09/17/837- ikea-maintains-china-expansion-plans/ (accessed December 10, 2008). Paul M. Miller, "IKEA with Chinese Characteristics," *China Business Review*, http://www.chinabusinessreview.com/public/0407/company_ profile.html, (accessed December 10, 2008).

82. Shaun Rein, interview by author, Shanghai, China, August 27, 2007. "China's Stimulus Package: Will It Work, and What's Next?" Knowledge@Wharton, November 19, 2008, http://www.knowl- edgeatwharton.com.cn/index.cfm?fa=viewfeature&languageid=1&articl eid=1954, (accessed December 10, 2008).

83. China's contribution to global economic growth exceeded that of the United States for the first time in 2007, accounting for 27 percent of global growth. "Stronger China," *Economist*, September 27, 2007. "Obama Needs Time to Rescue U.S. Economy," *Irish Times*, November 11, 2008, http://www.irishtimes.com/newspaper/opinion/2008/1111/1225925652906.html (accessed December 15, 2008).

84. Japan's economy was valued at about $1.28 trillion in the second quarter of 2010, slightly below China's $1.33 trillion.

85. The U.S.-China Business Council, "U.S. Exports to China, 2000-2007," U.S. Department of Commerce, U.S. International Trade Commission, 2008, http://www.uschina.org/public/exports/us_exports_to_china_2007.pdf (accessed December 13, 2008) and http://www.uschina.org/statistics/tradetable.html (accessed December 9, 2009).

86. Paul Gao, "A Global Road Map for China's Automakers," *McKinsey Quarterly*, June 2008, http://www.mckinseyquarterly.com/A_global_road_map_for_Chinas_automakers_2137_abstract (accessed June 29, 2008). Florian Bressand, et al., "Leapfrogging to Higher Energy Productivity in China," McKinsey Global Institute, June 2007.

87. "General Motors Sets Sales Record in China in 2011," *GM News*, Jan. 8, 2012, http://media.gm.com/content/media/us/en/gm/news.detail.html/content/Pages/news/us/en/2012/Jan/0109_Sales_China (accessed April 4, 20012).

88. David Barboza and Nick Bunkley, "G.M., Eclipsed at Home, Soars to Top in China," *New York Times*, July 21, 2010.

89. Keith Naughton, "The Great Wal-Mart of China," *Newsweek*, October 30, 2006.

90. Carol Matlack, "Auchan: Wal-Mart's Tough New Global Rival," *Businessweek*, October 23, 2009.

91. "Interview with Warren Liu, Author of 'KFC in China: Recipe for Success,'" July 2, 2009, http://seekingalpha.com/article/146569-interview-with-warren-liu-author-of-kfc-in-china-recipe-for-success (accessed December 9, 2009).

92. "Coming of Age: Multinational Companies in China," an *Economist* Intelligence Unit white paper in cooperation with Citigroup, DHL, KPMG, and Monitor Group, *Economist*, June 2004.

93. Michael Bloomberg, "A Race We Can All Win," *Newsweek*, Dec. December 22, 2007, http://www.newsweek.com/id/81592 (accessed. August 5, 2008).

94. Pew Research Center, "U.S. Seen as Less Important, China as More Powerful," Pew Global Attitudes Project, December 3, 2009, http://people-press.org/report/569/americas-place-in-the-world (accessed April 20, 2010).

95. World Bank, http://en.wikipedia.org/wiki/List_of_countries_by_GDP_%28nominal%29_per_capita.

96. "The Global 2000," Special Report, *Forbes*, April 8, 2009.

97. Joseph Nye, "China"s Century Is Not Yet Upon Us," Harvard Kennedy School, May 18, 2010, http://www.hks.harvard.edu/news-events/news/commentary/chinas-century-not-upon-us.

98. Stratfor, "China's Push to Increase Private Spending," January 31, 2008, http://www.stratfor.com/analysis/chinas_push_increase_private_spending (accessed December 10, 2008). Embassy of People's Republic of China in the Republic of Albania, "China's Economy 2007," http://al.china-embassy.org/eng/zggk/t514666.htm (accessed December 10, 2008).

99. "Round and Round It Goes," *Economist*, October 24-31, 2009.

100. U.S. Department of Commerce, Bureau of Economic Analysis, http://www.bea.gov. The personal saving rate was below 1% for the period 2005-2008.

101. U.S. Census Bureau, Foreign Trade Statistics, Trade in Goods (Imports, Exports, and Balance) with China, http://www.census.gov/foreign-trade/balance/c5700.html#2011.

102. U.S. Census Bureau, Foreign Trade Statistics, Trade in Goods (Imports, Exports, and Balance) with China, http://www.census.gov/foreign-trade/balance/c5700.html#2011.

103. Joseph Stiglitz, "World Has Much to Learn from China's New Economic Model," *Nation*, April 16, 2007. Michael Spence, "We are All in It Together," *Wall Street Journal*, January 5, 2007.
China-U.S. Center for Sustainable Development, 2004 China Gallup Poll.

104. Jonathan Woetzel, Janamitra Devan, et al., "Preparing for China's Urban Billion," McKinsey Global Institute, March 2008.

105. Chris Buckley, "China Report Warns of Greenhouse Gas Leap," Reuters, October 22, 2008. China is first in total emissions, but is significantly lower than the United States when measured per capita.

106. Spencer Swartz and Shai Oster, "China Tops U.S. in Energy Use," *Wall Street Journal*, July 18, 2010.

107. Joseph Kahn and Jim Yardley, "As China Roars, Pollution Reaches Deadly Extremes," *New York Times*, August 26, 2007.

108. Jonathan Woetzel, Janamitra Devan, et al., "Preparing for China's Urban Billion," McKinsey Global Institute, March 2008.

109. Keith Bradsher, "China Fears Consumer Impact on Global Warming," *New York Times*, July 4, 2010.

110. Keith Bradsher and David Barboza, "Pollution from Chinese Coal Casts a Global Shadow," *New York Times*, June 11, 2006.

111. Joseph Kahn and Jim Yardley, "As China Roars, Pollutions Reaches Deadly Extremes," *New York Times*, August 26, 2007.

112. "China Promises 1.35% of GDP as Annual Environmental Protection Investment," Xinhua, November 26, 2007, http://news.xinhuanet.com/english/2007-11/26/content_7150303.htm (accessed December 22, 2008).

113. "Cost of Pollution in China," World Bank, July 2007, World Bank, "Statement from World Bank China Country Director on 'Cost of Pollution in China' Report," Washington, D.C., July 11, 2007, http://web.worldbank.org/WBSITE/EXTERNAL/COUNTRIES/EASTASIAPACIFICEXT/EXTEAPREGTOPENVIRONMENT/0,,contentMDK:21406465~menuPK:502892~pagePK:2865114~piPK:2865167~theSitePK:502886,00.html (accessed December 20, 2008).

114. Mary-Anne Toy, "Pollution Facts Suppressed by China," *Sydney Morning Herald*, July 5, 2007, http://www.smh.com.au/news/world/pollution-facts-suppressed-by-china-pollution-facts-suppressed-bychina/2007/07/05/1183351302562.html# (accessed December 28, 2009).

115. "Cost of Pollution in China," World Bank, July 2007, World Bank, "Statement from World Bank China Country Director on 'Cost of

Pollution in China' Report," Washington, D.C., July 11, 2007, http://web.worldbank.org/WBSITE/EXTERNAL/COUNTRIES/EASTASIAPACIFICEXT/EXTEAPREGTOPENVIRONMENT/0,,contentMDK:21406465~menuPK:502892~pagePK:2865114~piPK:2865167~theSitePK:502886,00.html (accessed December 20, 2008).

116. Jacques Leslie, "The Last Empire: China's Pollution Problem Goes Global," *Mother Jones*, December 10, 2007. The Climate Group, "China's Clean Revolution," August 2008, www.theclimategroup.org.

117. "Cost of Pollution in China," World Bank, July 2007, World Bank, "Statement from World Bank China Country Director on 'Cost of Pollution in China' Report," Washington, D.C., July 11, 2007, http://web.worldbank.org/WBSITE/EXTERNAL/COUNTRIES/EASTASIAPACIFICEXT/EXTEAPREGTOPENVIRONMENT/0,,contentMDK:21406465~menuPK:502892~pagePK:2865114~piPK:2865167~theSitePK:502886,00.html (accessed December 20, 2008).

118. The Climate Group, "China's Clean Revolution," August 2008, www.theclimategroup.org.

119. Keith Bradsher and David Barboza, "Pollution from Chinese Coal Casts a Global Shadow," *New York Times*, June 11, 2006.

120. The Climate Group, "China's Clean Revolution," August 2008, www.theclimategroup.org.

121. Weston Sedgwick, "First Solar: 1 Billion Watts in 2009," Green Tech Daily.com, December 16, 2009, "One gigawatt of solar modules produces enough electricity to serve the needs of approximately 145,000 average American homes and saves roughly 1 million metric tons of carbon dioxide emissions annually," http://www.greentechnologydaily.com/solar-wind/543-first-solar-1-billion-watts-in-2009 (accessed June 7, 2010).

122. Keith Bradsher and David Barboza, "Pollution from Chinese Coal Casts a Global Shadow," *New York Times*, June 11, 2006.

123. Lou Schwartz, China Stategies, LLC, "China Renewable Energy and Sustainable Development Report," November 2007, http://www.renewableenergyaccess.com/assets/documents/2007/November_China_Renewable_Report.doc (accessed March 31, 2008).

124. "China Promises 1.35% of GDP as Annual Environmental Protection Investment," Xinhua, November 26, 2007, http://news.xinhuanet.com/english/2007-11/26/content_7150303.htm (accessed December 22, 2008).

125. Joseph Kahn and Jim Yardley, "As China Roars, Pollution Reaches Deadly Extremes," *New York Times*, August 26, 2007.

126. "Pathways to a Low-Carbon Economy: Version 2 of the Global Greenhouse Gas Abatement Cost Curve," McKinsey & Co., January 2009.

127. Li Fangfang, "Subsidy Will Help Plug-in Hybrid Sales, BYD Says," *China Daily*, August 18, 2009. "China Set to Lead in 'New Energy' Car Production," *China Stakes*, May 4, 2009, http://www.chinastakes.com/2009/5/china-set-to-lead-in-new-energy-car-production.html.

128. Marc Gunther, "Warren Buffett Takes Charge," *Fortune*, April 13, 2009. "China Set to Lead in 'New Energy' Car Production," *China Stakes*, May 4, 2009, http://www.chinastakes.com/2009/5/china-set-to-lead-in-new-energy-car-production.html.

129. Xin Jin, interview by author, Cupertino, California, , September 4, 2009.

130. "China to Pay Subsidies for EVs, Plug-in Hybrids," Associated Press, June 1, 2010.

131. "Global Automotive Industry Gets US$44 Billion Boost from Governments for Alternative Fuel Technologies," Deloitte, http://www.deloitte.com/view/en_CN/cn/press/cn-pressreleases-en/8f31c690e9429210VgnVCM200000bb42f00aRCRD.htm (accessed July 12, 2010).

132. Jonathan Woetzel, "China and the U.S.: The Potential of a Clean-tech Partnership," *McKinsey Quarterly*, August 2009.

133. National Bureau of Statistics, China Statistic Yearbook (2007), Jianzhu ye fang shi jian zhu mian zhi (Construction Area of the Building Industry), Zhongguo jie neng wang, Zhongguo dui xin jian jian zhu cai qu qiang zhi xing jie neng cuo shi (China's Strong Energy Efficiency Measures Towards Promotion of Efficiency in New Construction), Zhongguo jie neng wang, November 20, 2007.

134. Li Yue, interview by author, May 15, 2008.

135. Rob Watson, interview by author, Palo Alto, California, April 24, 2008.

136. Jin Ruidong, interview by author, Beijing, China, May 29, 2008. All units have been changed from square meters to square feet.

137. Florian Bressand, Diana Farrell, et al., "Leapfrogging to Higher Energy Productivity in China," McKinsey Global Institute, June 2007.

138. David Nieh, interview by author, Shanghai, China, June 7, 2008.

139. Wang Miansheng, interview by author, Oregon, April 17, 2008.

140. Rob Watson, interview by author, Palo Alto, California, April 24, 2008.

141. Keith Bradsher, "China Drawing High-Tech Research from U. S.," *New York Times*, March 17, 2010.

142. Li Yiyu, "Smart Grid Project Generates Local Buzz," *China Daily*, June, 10, 2010.

143. Jeff Siegel, "Will China Control Smart Grid Too?" Green Chip Stocks, Chinese Smart Grid, http://www.greenchipstocks.com/articles/chinese-smart-grid/991 (accessed July 12, 2010).

144. Kenneth G. Lieberthal, "Overcoming Obstacles to U.S.-China Cooperation on Climate Change," Brookings Institution, February 24, 2009.

145. "China's Clean Revolution II," Climate Group, August 2009, www.the-climategroup.org.

146. Tang Man-chung, interview by author, Chongqing, China, May 13, 2008.

147. In a cap-and-trade program, the government provides permits to companies that limit a company's allowed emissions, while capping total emissions. The government allows a company to sell (trade) its permits to other companies, as long as the company does not need the permits for its own emissions. In this way, total emissions are capped, and companies are allowed to trade emissions permits according to their needs.

148. Jamie P. Horsley, "Village Elections: Training Ground for Democratization," *China Business Review*, March-April 2001. Jemie P. Horsley is lawyer and consultant to the Carter Center's China Village Election Project. She lived and worked in China for thirteen years.

149. Wang Jun (name is changed to protect his identity), interviewed by author at Shanghai Pudong International Airport, June 8, 2008.

150. *South Wind View*, special edition, October 16, 2007, p. 22 (translated by author).

151. Jonathan D. Spence, *The Search for Modern China*, Second Edition (W. W. Norton & Company, ew York: 1999). Wikipedia, The Free Encyclopedia,

181. As quoted by Sonia Kolesnikov-Jessop, "Spotlight: Jack Ma, cofounder of Alibaba.com Business—*International Herald Tribune*," *New York Times*, January 5, 2007.

182. As quoted by Susan Kuchinskas, "Jack Ma, CEO, Alibaba," www.internetnews.com, October 22, 2004.

183. As quoted by John Heilemann, "Unlocking the Middle Kingdom," *Business 2.0*, August 2006.

184. As quoted by Jason Dean and Jonathan Cheng, "Meet Jack Ma, Who Will Guide Yahoo! In China," *Wall Street Journal* (Eastern Edition), August 12, 2005, p. B1.

185. Mylene Mangalindan, "China May Be eBay's Latest Challenge as Local Rivals Eat into Market Share," *Wall Street Journal* (Eastern Edition), October 12, 2006, p. C1.

186. Mary Meeker, Lina Choi, Yoshiko Motoyama, "The China Internet Report," Morgan Stanley Equity Research, April 14, 2004.

187. As quoted by Justin Doebele, "Standing Up to eBay," *Forbes* 175, no. 8 (April 18, 2005): p. 50.

188. Mylene Mangalindan, "China May Be eBay's Latest Challenge as Local Rivals Eat Into Market Share." The Wall Street Journal (Eastern Edition). New York, N.Y.: Oct 12, 2006. pg. C.1.

189. David Barboza, "Improbable Saga of China's New Internet King," *New York Times*, August 16, 2005.

190. "Business: China's Pied Piper; Face Value," *Economist* 380, No. 8496 (September 23, 2006), p. 80.

191. "E-commerce Key to China Web Growth," CNN.com, October 19, 2005, http://edition.cnn.com/2005/Tech/10/19/spark.jack.ma/index.html (accessed October 23, 2007).

192. Clay Chandler, Asia editor, "Open Sesame for China's Web King," *Fortune*, November 25, 2007.

193. Vivian Wai-yin Kwok, "Alibaba Said to Plan Overseas IPO for B2B Unit," *Forbes*, May 1, 2007.

194. As quoted in BMPC, "Interviews with Alibaba.com's CEO, Jack Ma," http://resources.alibaba.com (accessed February 2, 2007).

195. "Jack Ma TalkAsia Transcript," CNN.com, April 25, 2006, http://edition.cnn.com/2006/WORLD/asiapcf/04/24/talkasia.ma.script/index.html (accessed December 6, 2008).

196. Yolanda Wang, Veronica Chen, and Rebecca Zhang, interview by author, Shanghai, China, June 3, 2008.

197. Shi Jingfeng, interview by author, Shanghai, China, June 6, 2008.

198. "Religion in China on the Eve of the 2008 Beijing Olympics," Pew Forum, May 2, 2008, http://pewforum.org/docs/?DocID=301 (accessed September 8, 2008).

199. Shi Yu, "300 Million Religious Adherents in China," *Epoch Times*, February 25, 2007, http://en.epochtimes.com/news/7-2-15/51698.html (accessed July 19, 2010).

200. Slavoj Zizek, "How China Got Religion," *International Herald Tribune*, October 11, 2007.

201. Bill Smith, "West's Shangri-la Fantasy Creates 'Virtual Tibet' Uprising and the Dalai Lama's Flight into Exile," Monsters and Critics, March 9, 2009, http://www.monstersandcritics.com/news/asiapacific/features/article_1463485.php/Wests_Shangri-la_fantasy_creates_&quotVirtual_Tibet&quot_uprising_and_the_Dalai_Lamas_flight_into_exile_Feature_#ixzz09HSjBjSy (accessed July 19, 2010).

202. "Sons of Heaven: Christianity in China," *Economist*, October 4-10, 2008.

203. "When Opium Can Be Benign," *Economist*, February 1, 2007.

204. "Religion in China on the Eve of the 2008 Beijing Olympics," Pew Forum, May 2, 2008, http://pewforum.org/docs/?DocID=301 (accessed September 8, 2008).

205. Dong Lu, interview by author, Beijing, China, May 27, 2008.

206. Shi Jingfeng, interview by author, Shanghai, China, June 6, 2008.

207. The poem is translated by author.

208. As quoted by Jonathan D. *Spence, The Search for Modern China, Second Edition (New York: W. W. Norton & Company, 1999), p. 256.*

209. Chen Yuqing, "The Power of Love," *Harper's Bazaar*, Chinese Edition, March 2008.

ACKNOWLEDGMENTS

I owe many debts of gratitude in writing this book. The first and foremost person I want to thank is my husband, who believed in me before I believed in myself. He has lived through every moment of this book. He is not only an enthusiastic supporter, but also an excellent sounding board. His love and faith in me have made many difficult times in writing more endurable. Without his constant encouragement and tireless editing, this book could not have been completed.

I want to thank my agent, John Willig, who took a risk on a first time author. I owe thanks to my editor Johanna Vondeling and the entire team at Berrett-Koehler, who provided important guidance and support when the book's initial arguments were being developed. I want to thank Sharon Goldinger, whose masterful skills of editing made the first drafts of the manuscript more manageable, and Hillel Black, who not only edited this book, but also championed it. I owe thanks to Po Bronson, the New York Times best-selling author, who kindly mentored me throughout the long writing process.

Many academics and industry professionals helped illuminate for me topics related to China. Michael Spence, the Nobel prize winning economist, generously offered insights about China's economic growth. James Fallows, national correspondent for the *Atlantic*, enlightened me on many topics on China. Professor William F. Miller at Stanford gave me helpful advice. Shaun Rein, founder and managing director of China Market Research Group (CMR), supported this project throughout. And there were many others who helped during the process.

I am indebted to many people who graciously introduced their friends and family members in China for me to interview. Among them are my dear friends Lixin Chen, Vida Zhang Fargis, Bing Wei Edwards, and many more. Their friendship and support mean the world to me. I want to thank Deng Feng, who kindly brainstormed ideas for the book with me despite his busy schedule, Jin Yi, who is an energetic supporter, and Tina Shi, who connected me to key people in China. Wang Jianshuo introduced me to many interesting people, some of whom were featured in the book. Laurie Duthie not only introduced me to her friends in Wuhan, but also generously shared her paper about white collars in China. Bill Li shared his invaluable insights and wisdom on many subjects. Other people who helped along the way are Bill McEwen of Gallup, Vincent Lo of Shui On Land, Porter Erisman of Alibaba, Barbara Finamore of Natural Resources Defense Council, Lonnie Hodge in Guangzhou, professor Zhu Yinghuang in Beijing, Steve Musheroo, Patricia Clarke, Man-chung Tang, Toni Wyncoop, Ann Xing, Ge Zhenzhou, John Chiang, Tarry Mahony, Prashant Loyalka, Charles Wang, Yolanda Wang, Cai Lily, Zhou Junjian, and more.

I owe many thanks to my excellent peers and reviewers. Adam Tolnay, my colleague at the Stanford fellowship program, provided helpful comments. Gady Epstein, *Forbes* Beijing Bureau Chief, took time from his extremely busy schedule to review the manuscript and provide invaluable feedback. Martha Bullen helped crystallize the chapter summaries. Davis Fields gave great suggestions to clarify the positioning of the book. Other people who reviewed the manuscript and provided helpful feedback include Caitlin Kelly-Sneed, Bill Dodson, Jihong Sanderson, Carlos Soto, and Robert Elliott. People who kindly offered to review the manuscript are Jeremy Goldkorn, founder of the popular blog site danwei.org, Joel Dreyfuss, former editor-in-chief of Red Herring, Ray Kwong, marketing guru and business advisor, and Jill Buck, Founder and Executive Director of Go Green Initiative and Host of Go Green Radio.

Finally yet importantly, I owe infinite thanks to the hundreds of people I talked to in China who are the subject of this book. Without them, and their generosity in spending time with me and answering my questions, this book would never have been written.

Helen H. Wang
California, U. S. A.
August 2010

INDEX

ABOUT THE AUTHOR

Helen Wang is a *Forbes* columnist and consultant on China's middle class. Originally from China, Wang has lived in the United States for over twenty years. After finishing her master's degree at Stanford University, she joined a prestigious think tank, Institute for the Future, in Menlo Park, California, and consulted for Fortune 500 companies, including Apple Computer, Oracle, and Bank of America. Wang then became an entrepreneur in Silicon Valley Internet start-ups. In 2004, she returned to Stanford University as a Reuters Fellow, developing technology solutions for underserved communities. Wang has appeared on BBC World Television News, CNNMoney, been quoted by the Wall Street Journal, The Christian Science Monitor, and featured in San Jose Mercury News, China Daily, and other major media. A sought-after speaker, Wang now divides her time between consulting for companies doing business in China and helping nonprofit organizations make a difference. She lives in Silicon Valley with her husband, her dog Frodo, and her parakeets.

http://TheHelenWang.com

CPSIA inform
Printed in the
LVOW11s172
4922781